JACKIE ROBINSON

BREAKING BARRIERS IN BASEBALL

>>TRAIL BLAZERS

Neil Armstrong

Jackie Robinson

Harriet Tubman

Jane Goodall

>>TRAIL BLAZERS

JACKIE ROBINSON

BREAKING BARRIERS IN BASEBALL

KURTIS SCALETTA

RANDOM HOUSE 🏠 NEW YORK

Text copyright © 2019 by Kurtis Scaletta
Cover art copyright © 2019 by Luisa Uribe and George Ermos
Interior illustrations copyright © 2019 by Artful Doodlers
Trailblazers logo design by Mike Burroughs

Visit us on the Web! rhcbooks.com

Educators and librarians, for a variety of teaching tools, visit us at
RHTeachersLibrarians.com

Library of Congress Cataloging-in-Publication Data
Name: Scaletta, Kurtis, author.
Title: Jackie Robinson: breaking barriers in baseball / by Kurtis Scaletta.
Other titles: Trailblazers: Jackie Robinson
Description: First edition. | New York: Random House, [2019] | Series: Trailblazers |
Audience: Ages: 8 to 12. | Includes index.
Identifiers: LCCN 2019010628 (print) | LCCN 2019014036 (ebook) | ISBN 978-0-593-12404-8
(trade pbk.) | ISBN 978-0-593-12405-5 (lib. bdg.) | ISBN 978-0-593-12406-2 (ebook)
Subjects: LCSH: Robinson, Jackie, 1919–1972—Juvenile literature. | African American baseball
players—Biography—Juvenile literature. | Baseball players—United States—
Biography—Juvenile literature.
Classification: LCC GV865.R6 (ebook) | LCC GV865.R6 S28 2019 (print) |
DDC 796.357092 [B]—dc23

Created by Stripes Publishing Limited, an imprint of the Little Tiger Group

Printed in the United States of America
10 9 8 7 6 5 4 3 2 1

First Edition

Contents

Introduction   **1**
"If I Make Good"

Chapter 1   **13**
Growing Up Black in White America

Chapter 2   **31**
A Way Out

Chapter 3   **49**
A Rising Star

Chapter 4   **67**
Change Comes to Baseball

Chapter 5   **85**
The Loneliest Man in Sports

Chapter 6   **101**
A World Series Victory

Chapter 7   **123**
Life After Baseball

Conclusion   **137**
A Legacy

Timeline   **150**

Further Reading   **154**

Glossary   **156**

Index   **160**

"IF I MAKE GOOD"

One of the most important plays in baseball history was a ground ball to third base. It was April 15, 1947: opening day at Ebbets Field, home of the Brooklyn Dodgers. A rookie named Jackie Robinson came to the plate and bounced the ball to the left side of the infield. The Boston Braves third baseman fielded the ball and threw it to first as Jackie reached the base. The fans thought Jackie had gotten to the base before the ball, but the umpire signaled an out.

Jackie hits the ball.

The third baseman throws to first.

Will Jackie get there in time?

He's out!

"We was robbed!" Dodgers fans bellowed from the stands.

Jackie turned to glare at the umpire. For a moment it looked as if he were going to argue the call. Instead, he retreated to the dugout. It didn't make much of a difference in the game, but it was the first time a black player had swung a bat in Major League Baseball in almost sixty years.

A GENTLEMAN'S AGREEMENT

Jackie Robinson was not the first black player in the major leagues. There were a few in the very early days of baseball.

WILLIAM EDWARD WHITE
First Base

- Providence Grays (one game), 1879
- First known player of African descent who played Major League Baseball, 40 years before Jackie Robinson was born

WILLIAM EDWARD WHITE
First Base

MOSES FLEETWOOD WALKER
Catcher

- Toledo Blue Stockings, 1884. Walker's brother, Welday, played 5 games that same season as an outfielder.
- Newark Little Giants, 1887

MOSES FLEETWOOD WALKER
Catcher

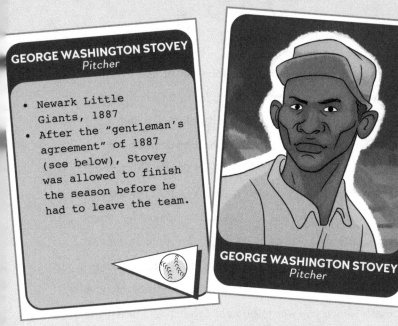

GEORGE WASHINGTON STOVEY
Pitcher

- Newark Little Giants, 1887
- After the "gentleman's agreement" of 1887 (see below), Stovey was allowed to finish the season before he had to leave the team.

GEORGE WASHINGTON STOVEY
Pitcher

Those were the wild and woolly early days of baseball. New teams came along every year, and other teams folded. Teams changed names and cities so often, it was hard to keep up! Entire leagues could rise to major-league status and then fall back to the minors a few years later. The rules were always changing. It took six or seven balls for a walk, instead of four, and foul balls didn't count as strikes.

There was never an official rule against black players in organized baseball, but in 1887, team owners came to what was called a "gentleman's agreement." They decided no major- or minor-league team would sign another black player.

So, before the baseball establishment had even agreed on how many balls made up a walk, it had decided the game was for white players only.

Over the next sixty years, baseball grew as the national pastime. Ty Cobb of the Detroit Tigers and later Babe Ruth of the New York Yankees were the country's biggest heroes. Baseball stadiums became the beating hearts of most major American cities. And baseball became a big business! Larger stadiums were built so more fans could come to watch the excitement. Everywhere you went you heard the cheers and groans of games booming out of radio sets, or people talking about the local team at bus stops and cafés. By the mid-1940s, some games were on television.

Black players had their own teams and leagues but played in the shadows of organized baseball. The Negro League schedules and scores were usually not printed in the daily newspaper. The games were rarely broadcast on the radio. There was certainly no talk of televising them.

As unfair as that was, organized baseball was no different from many other institutions in America. Most of the country was deeply segregated, meaning that people of different racial backgrounds lived very separate lives.

Segregation

This segregation could be seen across all areas of life:

- Most white children had few or no black children in their classes and never had a black teacher.

- White patients never had a black doctor or a black nurse.

- White passengers on a bus or train never had a black driver.

- White moviegoers saw black actors playing only minor roles.

So it did not seem unusual to white spectators at a ballpark that they never saw a black player take the field.

⩵ MR. RICKEY'S NOBLE EXPERIMENT ⩵

During World War II, over a million black men and women served in the US military—including Jackie Robinson. Many fought and died for their country. Black Americans had shown courage and sacrifice, many white people realized, and deserved access to the American dream. Meanwhile, factories had hired blacks to work alongside whites to keep up with the demands of the war. It had worked on the factory floor—why not in baseball?

Of course, some groups, such as the National Association for the Advancement of Colored People (NAACP), had been trying for decades to win justice for black Americans. Their goal was integration, meaning black people could live in the same neighborhoods, go to the same schools, and have the same job opportunities as white people did. But it wasn't until after World War II that those efforts started to pay off.

The president and co-owner of the Brooklyn Dodgers at the time was Branch Rickey. Rickey had been a baseball executive for thirty years. He helped build championship teams in St. Louis before moving to Brooklyn.

His three favorite pursuits were:

1) doing the right thing

2) winning baseball games

3) making money

Rickey knew that bringing top talent from the Negro Leagues to the Dodgers would help him do all three at once. But he had to sign the perfect player to do it. He decided on Jackie Robinson. Jackie was not the best player in the Negro Leagues, but Rickey liked his seriousness and discipline. He liked that Jackie had gone to college and had served his country. Rickey brought Jackie to New York, saying that he was starting a new Negro League team. Once Jackie was in his office, Branch told him the truth. He wanted Jackie to play for the Dodgers!

Branch Rickey warned him that it wouldn't be easy and that Jackie would have people yelling at him and calling him names. He told Jackie that if he let these actions get to him, or yelled, or called others names in return, people would say black ballplayers didn't belong in Major League Baseball. If Jackie was a victim of a bad call, he couldn't complain to the umpire. If he was treated unfairly, he couldn't grumble to the newspapers. Jackie Robinson promised he would try.

As he walked to the dugout after his first plate appearance as a Dodger in 1947, Jackie kept his promise to Branch Rickey and to himself. He would not make waves.

He did not get a hit that day, but he drew a walk late in the game, stole second base, and then ran to third on an error. From there he scored the game-winning run. When he left the ballpark to catch a train back to his hotel, fans—white and black—surrounded him, eager to shake hands with the newest Dodger.

Jackie downplayed the significance of the game to the newspapers. He knew it was a historic moment, but he also knew that the white newspapers would make too much of it if he came across as arrogant or self-important.

Jackie Robinson had crossed baseball's color line, but his journey was just beginning. He had played one game in front of a friendly crowd. He knew he would face bigger challenges on the road. He knew he would be mistreated by crowds in other ballparks. He knew that he would be barred from many of the restaurants and hotels other players enjoyed. He knew white reporters would watch him, waiting for him to blow his top or muff a play so they could say the experiment was a failure.

He knew he must shoulder the big load without cracking, and not just to save his own spot on the team. He had to do it to open the door for other talented black baseball players and to prove to America that integration would work.

On that chilly afternoon of his first game, Jackie didn't know if he'd even make it through the season. He certainly didn't know that someday he'd be one of the game's best-ever players! On April 15, 1947, Jackie Robinson might have known only one thing: he would not keep silent forever. One day he would speak his mind.

APRIL 16, 1947

ROBINSON
BREAKS BARRIER

APRIL 16,

JACKIE SCORES
WINNING RUN

APRIL 16,

ROBINSON MAKES
MAJOR-LEAGUE DEBUT

CHAPTER 1

GROWING UP BLACK IN WHITE AMERICA

Jack Roosevelt Robinson was born on January 31, 1919, a few miles from Cairo, Georgia. Though the world would later know him as Jackie, he never used the name himself—he was always Jack. His parents chose his middle name in honor of Theodore "Teddy" Roosevelt, who had died earlier that month. As President, Roosevelt spoke out against racism, inspiring and encouraging many families across America.

Theodore Roosevelt

Slavery had ended over fifty years earlier in Georgia, but in lots of ways the rural South went on as if nothing had changed. Black people usually lived in poverty and had few jobs open to them. Laws told them where they could go to school, even where they could use the bathroom or get a drink of water. The many laws that kept blacks separate—or segregated—and second-class were called Jim Crow laws.

⟩ JIM CROW LAWS ⟨

Each state had its own set of laws, but in all the former Confederate states there were rules for keeping black people and white people apart. Some of the laws in Georgia included:

Jim Crow Laws

- Schools shall not admit both white and black children, or they will lose funding.

- Marriage between a black person and a white person is strictly forbidden. If such a marriage happens, the husband and wife as well as the person issuing the marriage certificate and the minister conducting the service will be fined and go to jail.
- Black and white passengers shall not ride, dine, or sleep in the same railway car. Trains are not required to provide sleeping or dining accommodations to black passengers.
- Public places must provide separate restrooms and drinking fountains for white people and black people.
- Restaurants and hotels may serve either white people or black people but not both.

Jackie was the youngest of five children. His parents, Jerry and Mallie, were sharecroppers; they farmed but didn't own the land. They worked for a white landowner, growing peanuts, cotton, sugar cane, and vegetables.

When Jackie was not even a year old , his father took some money and said he was going into town. Jackie would never see or hear from him again. Mallie knew she could never handle the farm and five children all by herself.

FROM CAIRO TO CALIFORNIA

But Mallie's brother Burton had moved to California years before. He wrote letters to Mallie, telling her that there were plenty of jobs in California and that discrimination against black people was not as bad there. In one letter, he wrote:

So Mallie packed up their few belongings and spent their savings on train

If you want to get closer t heaven, come to California.

tickets to Los Angeles. The trip took almost two weeks.

At first the Robinsons shared an apartment with Uncle Burton. They lived in Pasadena, a city ten miles from Los Angeles. In 1920, Pasadena was the wealthiest city in the United States. It was also a sports lover's paradise! In the winter, people would travel to Pasadena to watch football games in its famous stadium, the Rose Bowl, or to play golf. With warm weather year-round, kids never needed to put away their baseball bats or soccer balls for the season.

Mallie found jobs cooking and cleaning for white families. She worked shorter days and made better money than she had in Georgia. After saving for three years, she and her brother bought a house at 121 Pepper Street. It was a white two-story house with four bedrooms and two baths—a mansion for a family that had always lived in cramped quarters.

But they were the only black people on the block, and not all the white residents were happy about their new neighbors. Some even tried to pool enough money to buy the house out from under them! But Mallie Robinson was practical. She shared baked goods with neighbors and made her older children do odd jobs for them. Soon the Robinsons had plenty of friends on the block, and there was no more talk about buying their house.

Jackie had three older brothers, and all of them enjoyed sports. His oldest brother, Edgar, loved to roller-skate and ride his bicycle.

Edgar

Mallie

Mack

He was so fast on skates, he would race the bus down the street and win. Another brother, Matthew (Mack), was a fast runner and dreamed of competing in the Olympics one day. Jackie looked up to his brothers, but he was closest to his sister, Willa Mae. She took care of him when their mother was at work. She bathed him and dressed him when he was a toddler, even though she wasn't much older than he was. When Jackie was too young for school, Willa Mae took him with her. The teachers allowed it, because they knew Mallie was a single parent and had to work.

$\stackrel{=}{\underset{\text{\tiny /}}{}}$ SCHOOL DAYS $\stackrel{=}{\underset{\text{\tiny \textbackslash}}{}}$

One of the reasons Mallie had moved her family to California was so they could get a better education. In Georgia, black children went to separate schools. They usually had fewer materials, bigger classes, and lower-paid teachers. In Pasadena, all kids went to the same schools.

Pasadena was not a paradise of equality, however. For example, all the teachers in Pasadena were white. Even if they tried to be fair, racial bias sometimes crept in. Report cards had suggestions for future careers. One of Jackie's report cards looked like this:

REPORT CARD

NAME: *Jack Robinson*

FUTURE CAREER: *Jack could become a gardener.*

One of the more common jobs for black men in Pasadena was tending gardens for wealthy families. It was work that didn't require much education. Jackie's teachers did not expect their black students to go to college—to become doctors or lawyers or teachers.

But Jackie's friends were different races. They were all poor, and they got along. The other kids did notice that Jackie didn't have a father, which was unusual, so they teased him about it. They also teased him because so many people lived in his house. Besides the six Robinsons, there were almost always other family members staying there: his uncle Burton and his aunt at first, and later various relatives from Georgia as they moved to California. Mallie would make room for them until they could get their own place. The house on Pepper Street was big, but it was always crowded.

Jackie never showed that the teasing hurt, but sometimes he went home sad and frustrated.

"Do you think our daddy will ever come back?" he asked his brothers and sister after being teased.

"We don't want him to find us," they told him. "He used to whip all of us. That's the reason Mommy doesn't want him back, or any other husband."

Jackie had no response to that. He didn't remember his father, or Georgia. He was still a baby when the family moved to California.

"Why does Mom have to let everybody stay here?" he sometimes complained. It meant he and Mack had to share a room. Worst of all, when his mother got cookies and cakes, she shared them with everyone in the neighborhood.

That's just the way Mom is— loving and kind.

Or maybe she's just soft.

≡ FAMILY BONDS ≡

When Jackie was eight, his grandmother came to live
with the Robinsons. Her face was a mass of wrinkles,
and her voice was harsh. She had been born in slavery
and told Jackie stories about what she had seen
and been through in her life. She talked about the
last days of slavery, saying that some black people
feared freedom. They had spent their whole lives
in slavery and didn't know how else to live. She had
also seen men and women broken by Jim Crow laws.
She reminded Jackie to keep his dignity, whatever
happened to him.

His grandmother left a deep impression on him.
She helped Jackie understand that his father was not
a bad man. He had left the family, but he'd suffered
through a life of poverty and unfairness. Jackie
never quite forgave his father, but he had a better
understanding of why he'd acted the way he did.

Jackie's grandmother also helped him appreciate
how strong his mother was. Mallie had never been
broken inside. She remained kind and loving to her
children and generous to her family from Georgia
and even to strangers.

⋸ SPORTS AND STONES ⋸

By kindergarten, Jackie was known for his skill at games. He was the marble champion of the neighborhood. He won at dodgeball so regularly, the school stopped playing it. Nobody could ever get him out!

It didn't matter what the game was: soccer, baseball, football, or a foot race. Jackie wanted in, and Jackie would win. He would agree to play on the same teams as other kids in exchange for small change or a share of their lunch.

Games didn't always keep Jackie out of trouble. One white family across the street was never won over by Mallie's kindness. They complained constantly about the Robinsons and called the police when Edgar rolled by the house on his skates. One day Jackie stepped outside, and a little girl who lived across the street called him a racist name. He called her a name right back. Her father joined in; soon they were hurling rocks instead of words. Jackie had good aim and a strong arm. He held his own in the battle with a grown man.

At last the man's wife came out and ended it. "Shame on you, throwing stones at a small child!" she told her husband.

Mallie came out and dragged Jackie inside. He was sure he'd get a scolding, but his mother told him she was proud of him. "You shouldn't throw stones at people," she said. "But you should always stand up for yourself when you're mistreated."

≥ THE PEPPER STREET GANG ≥

As he grew older, Jackie hung out with a group of kids who called themselves the Pepper Street Gang. They did not get into any serious trouble, but they sometimes stole fruit from vendors, threw clods of dirt at cars, and collected golf balls from the weeds of the golf course to sell back to their owners. The police got to know the boys, and they knew that Jackie Robinson was their unofficial leader. Just as there were no black teachers in Pasadena, there were no black police officers. Jackie and his friends often felt targeted.

Pasadena's public swimming pool, the Brookside Plunge, was open to non-white children only one day a week.

The pool called it "International Day" and promised white customers that the water would be changed at the end of the day.

One hot summer day, Jackie and his friends wanted to go swimming, and, as it was not a Tuesday, they set out for a dip in the public reservoir. They were caught by the police and taken to jail.

One of the boys said he was thirsty. The white policeman gave them all slices of watermelon and took photos as the boys ate it. It was humiliating. Jackie had seen illustrations of black people drawn with exaggerated features to make them look subhuman—in those pictures, they were always shown eating watermelon. The boys knew the police were using the watermelon to mock them. It was a blow to his dignity that Jackie would never forget.

Jackie and his friends were resentful about having to play by different rules than white kids. That led to more trouble with the Pepper Street Gang.

Sometimes Jackie would visit a car mechanic named Carl Anderson. Carl was a leader in the black community of Pasadena, and the boys looked up to him. One day Carl took Jackie aside. He'd heard about the Pepper Street Gang. He knew they only got into minor mischief, but he told Jackie he was headed down a dangerous road and was causing pain to his mother.

Jackie felt ashamed, thinking about all the sacrifices his mother had made. But he tried to act tough. He said he and his pals were just having fun. He said if he didn't go along with it, the others would think he was chicken. Carl told him it took more courage to go against the crowd.

Jackie shrugged and stalked away, not wanting to show Carl that his lecture had gotten to him. But he decided to stop getting into trouble from that day on.

I was too ashamed to tell Carl how right he was.

CHAPTER 2

A WAY OUT

The 1920s were a prosperous time in America, especially in Pasadena. The Robinson family did a little bit better every year, and things seemed to be looking up. That all changed on October 29, 1929, a day that would be called Black Tuesday.

OCTOBER 30, 1929

WALL STREET IN PANIC AS STOCKS CRASH

I HAVE 3 TRADES
I HAVE 3 CHILDREN
BUT I ONLY
WANT ONE JOB

Hard Times

During the 1920s, the economy in the United States had boomed, and people all over the country bought shares in flourishing companies, sometimes using credit from the banks. Stocks had become worth a lot more than the actual value of the companies. When the economy began to slow, stocks began to fall. In October of 1929, this decline made people panic. They began selling stocks like crazy.

This panic came to a head on Black Tuesday. The stock market lost about $30 billion in one day. Many people lost their life's savings. Businesses went broke and closed, leading to massive unemployment. Problems were worsened by widespread drought in the American Midwest; farmers lost their livelihoods, food prices rose. It was an extremely tough time that would become known as the:

GREAT DEPRESSION

Unemployed people flooded into California looking for work, competing for the kinds of jobs Mallie did. Families she worked for couldn't pay her anymore, or paid her less. Tourism in Pasadena dwindled, since fewer people could afford to travel.

Jackie's brothers Frank and Edgar, who were old enough to work, were unable to find regular jobs. It meant that Frank, who was now married, lived in the house on Pepper Street with his wife and two babies. Mallie had more mouths to feed. Sometimes the Robinsons lived on bread and water, and sometimes the sandwiches Jackie's friends shared with him were the only meal he'd get all day.

Jackie took odd jobs, watering lawns or selling snacks at sporting events, but the jobs never lasted long. He started to think about his future. He did not want to be a gardener, as his teacher had predicted. At the same time, he knew he might be lucky to be a gardener. He dreamed of getting a good job, one that he could use to help the entire family. He knew that college would be the best way to get a good job. But that led to two big questions. How would he get into a good college, and how would his family ever pay for it?

A NEW GAME PLAN

Living in Pasadena, home of the Rose Bowl, Jackie knew about college football. Unlike most professional sports, college football was not completely segregated. Some teams had a black player. Not all did, and there was almost never more than one black player on a team, but it was a chance for Jackie. Football could be a ticket to college, and college could be a ticket to a better life. Jackie also had his brother Mack as an example.

All his brothers were good at sports, but Mack was amazing. Mack poured everything he had into track and field, setting records in high school. In 1932, Los Angeles hosted the Summer Olympics. Mack tried out for the US team and didn't make it, but he was only eighteen years old. He resolved to work hard and compete in the next Olympics.

In junior high school, Jackie played football, basketball, and baseball, and competed in track and field.

Jackie did well in sports, but his teammates thought he was a show-off. Now that he was no longer spending as much time with the Pepper Street Gang, Jackie sometimes didn't feel like he had any friends. His older brother Frank coached him and gave him advice. He pointed out that Mack played hard and was headed for the Olympics. Jackie, Frank said, was also bound for glory.

"They're playing for fun, and you're playing for your future," he'd remind Jackie.

Jackie resolved to double down and try even harder. He wanted to be like Mack, and he didn't want to let Frank down.

Jackie was a fair student, earning B's and C's, but not a great one. He liked to read and was a regular at the library. Even though he didn't really enjoy school, he was eager to go to high school so that he could play sports at a higher level.

He transferred to the John Muir Technical High School as soon as he could, after turning sixteen, even though it was the middle of the school year. He won the starting shortstop position on the baseball team over older boys. He also made the track-and-field team, where he competed in the long jump and high jump.

In the fall he played football, and as soon as football was done, he tried out for basketball. When basketball was done, it was back to baseball. Jackie made an all-star baseball team that played in a tournament in Pomona.

Amazingly, that team included two other future Hall of Fame baseball players: Bob Lemon and Ted Williams. Unlike Jackie, Bob and Ted would be snapped up by baseball teams before they'd even graduated from high school. Jackie was as good as they were, but the color of his skin would keep him out of organized baseball for another ten years.

TED WILLIAMS
Outfielder

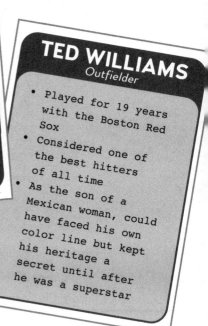

TED WILLIAMS
Outfielder

- Played for 19 years with the Boston Red Sox
- Considered one of the best hitters of all time
- As the son of a Mexican woman, could have faced his own color line but kept his heritage a secret until after he was a superstar

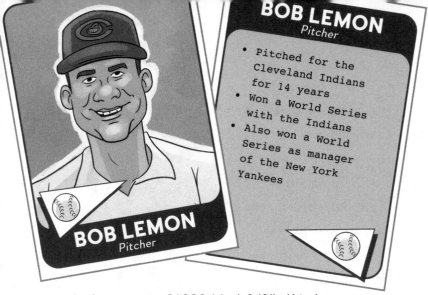

BOB LEMON
Pitcher

- Pitched for the Cleveland Indians for 14 years
- Won a World Series with the Indians
- Also won a World Series as manager of the New York Yankees

BOB LEMON
Pitcher

In the summer of 1936, Mack fulfilled his dream to compete in the Olympics, which were held in Berlin, Germany. Mack Robinson won a silver medal in the 200-meter dash, wearing worn-out shoes and having had little training. He would have set a world record and won the gold if it weren't for another black American athlete named Jesse Owens. Owens won four gold medals, one of the greatest Olympic achievements of all time. America cheered to see the black American defeat the white German athletes in front of Adolf Hitler, the leader of the Nazi party in Germany. Hitler believed that white people—especially white Germans—were better than everyone else and should be in charge. Jesse Owens's amazing performance proved to the world that the racist theories of Nazi Germany were wrong.

But America had racial issues of its own, and the way the country treated its Olympic heroes proved it. Jesse Owens, briefly the biggest sports star in the world, worked low-paying jobs and occasionally raced against horses as a sideshow attraction at fairs. Mack Robinson, who had finished a split second behind Owens, didn't come home to a hero's welcome or a single job offer. He became a street sweeper in Pasadena, wearing his official Olympic jacket on cold mornings.

⇒ A BREAKOUT YEAR ⇐

The next school year was a great one for Jackie. He
starred in four sports for the Muir Tech Terriers.

Jackie at John Muir Technical High School
1935–1937

→ **Baseball:** Jackie plays shortstop and catcher
and wins a spot on a regional all-star team.
→ **Football:** With Jackie as quarterback, the Terriers
win eighteen consecutive games. Jackie is known
for being able to run and pass for touchdowns.
→ **Basketball:** As the forward and team captain,
Jackie leads the team in scoring.
→ **Track and Field:** Jackie wins trophies for the
long jump and the high jump.

Like his brother Mack, Jackie found that his fame
disappeared the moment he was out of uniform. If
he went to a soda shop with black friends, they could
wait and wait and never get served. The movie theater
was segregated. Black families were not welcome at
the YMCA. Sometimes Jackie tested these limits—
changing seats in a dark theater or demanding service
when he was ignored at a diner. But he didn't make
serious trouble. For the most part, he was happy.

COLLEGE LIFE

Jackie turned eighteen midway through his senior year of high school. He left Muir Tech and enrolled at Pasadena Junior College (PJC), where his brother Mack attended. PJC was more integrated than most colleges. Even though there weren't very many black students, they could get fully involved in college life.

At first Jackie was known as Mack's kid brother. Mack was a big man on campus because of his accomplishments in track and field. But Jackie picked up right where he'd left off at Muir Tech, playing four sports.

Jackie at Pasadena Junior College
1937–1939

→ **Baseball:** Jackie plays as shortstop and is known for stealing bases and rattling pitchers. He doesn't hit for power but rarely strikes out.

→ **Football:** As quarterback on offense and safety on defense, Jackie scores touchdowns every possible way: running, passing, and returning interceptions and punts. He leads the team to sixteen consecutive wins.

→ **Basketball:** Jackie is the second-highest scorer in the league, trailing the leader by one point.

→ **Track and Field:** Jackie is still known as Mack's kid brother!

His success continued into summer, where he played for Pasadena's all-black Owl League—so-called because they played all their games at night. Jackie ran wild, stealing lots of bases.

Baseball Basics:
Stealing a Base

In baseball, a runner can wait safely on any base while his team continues to bat. A runner can also run to the next base—"steal" it—while the pitcher is pitching. The runner usually takes off as the pitcher goes into the windup or delivers the pitch. To foil the attempted steal, the catcher must catch the ball and throw it to the baseman, who must tag the runner before he reaches the base.

A runner who becomes caught in between bases and darts back and forth to avoid the tag is said to be in a "rundown," a "hot box," or a "pickle." Stealing home is the most difficult and daring move in baseball.

⋛ FAME AND MISFORTUNE ⋚

Newspaper reporters who wrote about Jackie praised his skill and his incredible feats, but tended to use words like *dusky* and *sepia* to describe him. Less subtle writers simply said Jackie had "very dark skin" or referred to him as "a colored boy." One, in the worst of racist depictions, said Robinson ran with the football like he'd stolen a watermelon from a farmer with a shotgun.

On the road, sometimes clerks refused Jackie a room in a hotel or waiters denied him service at a restaurant. A woman at a Sacramento restaurant told Jackie and another black player, Jack Gordon, "You can't eat here." The whole team walked out.

For the most part, Jackie tried not to let the mistreatment get to him, but he pushed back in small ways. When he noticed the black students at the integrated college retreating to the back of classrooms and auditoriums, Jackie encouraged them to spread out. When he took the bus, he refused to sit in the back. It wasn't required in California, as it was in other states, but many black riders did it out of habit.

Jackie also faced racism from his own teammates and from referees. The football team was mostly white, and most of the players accepted him—not just as a teammate but as a leader. He earned their respect with his skill, his drive to win, and his selfless style of play. But there were several players from Oklahoma who had followed Coach Tom Mallory from his previous job. They weren't comfortable with Jackie. They refused to talk to him or walked away when he approached.

Jackie remembered his mother's kindness to neighbors and how it ended most of the problems on Pepper Street. He made sure he gave the players the ball and a chance to score, and he was generous with compliments when they did well. He soon won them over.

Basketball, however, was a different story. Jackie and the other black players felt targeted by the all-white referees. The referees were quick to penalize Jackie on the court and even eject him from the game. Worse, they often failed to call blatant fouls against him, and he would leave the court bruised. The basketball team was struggling to win games, and having their star player limited or benched made it even harder. Jackie finally lost his temper.

After getting hit repeatedly in a game against Long Beach, with no effort by the refs to stop it, he hit back. The game fell apart as the two teams brawled, and some of the fans joined in. Long Beach students admitted that one of their own players had started the fight, but Jackie was branded as a troublemaker.

Jackie got into even deeper trouble off campus. Once, he and a friend were walking in downtown Pasadena, singing a popular jazz song called "Flat Foot Floogie." The term *flatfoot* was slang for a police officer, and a white policeman was offended. He confronted them, and Jackie unwisely argued back.

The policeman arrested both Jackie and his friend and took them to jail. The police denied them their "one phone call" and forced them to spend the night. Jackie was sentenced to ten days in jail, but the sentence was suspended—he could stay out of jail if he could stay out of trouble.

Even with his unfair reputation as a troublemaker, scouts from bigger colleges came to PJC football games to watch Jackie play. They offered him scholarships. Jackie thought about going to the University of Oregon, where his brother Mack had transferred. He settled on the University of California, Los Angeles. UCLA had one thing to offer that no other university could: it was close to home and to family. Jackie wanted the continued encouragement of his brother Frank.

CHAPTER 3

A RISING STAR

Jackie's brother Frank had been his biggest fan since junior high school. But just after Jackie started at UCLA, tragedy struck. Frank died in a motorcycle accident.

What will I do without his support?

A few months later, Jackie got in an argument with a white motorist, and once again he spent the night in jail. He pleaded guilty and was let off with a fine. Jackie knew coaches and college presidents were making appeals on his behalf, and even paying his fines. He was getting off easy because he was a sports star. But he also knew the trouble was caused by racist attitudes. He knew that young white men were never taken to jail for singing songs, getting into arguments, or swimming in a reservoir.

UCLA wanted to establish itself in sports by taking on the talented black athletes ignored by other schools. While other universities had black players, there were usually no more than two per team, and they were not allowed to outshine the white players. But the UCLA football team already had two black stars: running back Kenny Washington and receiver Woody Strode. After Robinson joined the UCLA Bruins, newspapers called them the:

"GOLD DUST TRIO"

GOLD DUST TRIO

That meant UCLA had three black players when there were fewer than forty in all of college football. Many of the black athletes on other teams would not get significant playing time, but the "Gold Dust Trio" would be the stars of their team.

The Bruins led off the season with two upset victories that raised Robinson to a new level of stardom. He was used to playing before five thousand fans; now he was playing before as many as a hundred thousand!

In his second game, played at the University of Washington, Jackie returned a sixty-five-yard punt for a touchdown, twisting and turning to slip past the defenders. That play won the game for the Bruins. Jackie played so well, even the Washington students stood up and cheered for him.

Jackie had a great season. He was still grieving his brother's death, and still resentful of his two run-ins with the law, but he had a rare ability that would make all the difference later in his career. Once he was playing, he could forget his troubles and think only of the game. In those early days at UCLA, newspapers—for reasons lost to history—started calling him Jackie. The nickname would stick and be his public name for the rest of his life.

Jackie had entered UCLA saying he would play
two sports: football—which brought the most
glory—and track and field. Track had never been his
best sport, but he hoped to compete in the 1940
Olympics. Those dreams were dashed when World
War II started and the Olympics were canceled. But
the basketball and baseball coaches at UCLA were
glad Jackie could help their teams.

Jackie at UCLA
1939-1941

→ **Football:** Jackie is called "the greatest ball carrier in the nation." In 1939, the Bruins go undefeated, though three games end in ties.

→ **Basketball:** Dazzling play by Jackie helps end a long losing streak by the Bruins but isn't enough to give them a winning season.

→ **Baseball:** Jackie once again plays short and gets a reputation for stealing bases but goes into a hitting slump he can't break out of.

→ **Track and Field:** Jackie sets a conference record and wins the NCAA title for the long jump.

→ **Combined:** Jackie is the first athlete at UCLA to "letter" in four sports—meaning he has significant playing time at the varsity level.

⇒ LOVE AND WAR ⇐

Jackie continued to shine in his second year at ULCA, but the football team and basketball team both had losing seasons. Something happened that was more important than sports or even his education. He met a student named Rachel Isum. Jackie was drawn to Rachel's intelligence and compassion.

At first, he later wrote, Jackie experienced a new kind of prejudice. Rachel Isum knew he was a star athlete and had seen him play. She was convinced he was cocky and full of himself. But as she got to know him, she learned Jackie had a serious mind and—more important—respected that she had one, too. After they'd known each other for a year, they were deeply in love.

> No matter what happens, this relationship is going to be one of the most important parts of my life.

Jackie began to wonder what he would do after college. The only thing he wanted to do was play sports, but there weren't many opportunities for black players to go pro in the sports he played. The National Football League had banned black players in 1933. The fledgling pro basketball leagues were all white. And baseball, of course, was segregated. But Jackie knew there were even fewer jobs for black men outside of sports, even with a college degree. He decided to leave college without graduating. His coaches, friends, and Rachel all tried to talk him out of it, but his mind was made up.

He took a job as an assistant athletic director with the National Youth Administration. He planned athletic activities for about a hundred boys. Most of those boys were white. It was unusual for a black man to oversee white youth, but Jackie connected with them. Like Jackie, many of them had grown up poor or without a father. He found the work challenging but rewarding. Unfortunately, the job didn't last long. After war erupted in Europe, the federal government shut down a lot of the Depression-era programs that helped people find work.

The Wartime Economy

The Depression was suddenly over as American industries experienced a wartime boom. The United States had not entered the war yet but was building ships and airplanes for the British, French, and Soviets—the group of countries known as the Allies.

The creation of more jobs meant new job opportunities for women and minorities. In 1941, President Franklin Roosevelt signed an executive order that US defense contractors could not discriminate based on race, religion, or national origin.

Jackie worked for a while at Lockheed Aircraft in Los Angeles and then played briefly in a semiprofessional football league in California. That job led to an opportunity to both play football and have a day job in Hawaii. He played football for the Honolulu Bears on Sundays and worked at a construction company the rest of the week in nearby Pearl Harbor.

The Honolulu Bears' season ended in November, and Jackie was homesick. He left Hawaii on December 5, 1941. Two days later, Pearl Harbor was bombed by the Imperial Japanese Army.

By the time Jackie's ship had reached the mainland, the United States was at war. Jackie had never considered a military career, but when he was drafted into the army in April he felt it was his duty to go.

SECOND LIEUTENANT JACKIE ROBINSON

Jackie was assigned to a base at Fort Riley, Kansas. The heavyweight boxing champion Joe Louis was assigned to the same army base. As a teenager, Jackie had listened to Joe's fights on the radio, bouncing around and shadowboxing along with the champion. Joe knew Jackie from his football days at UCLA. The two men became friends.

After basic training, Jackie applied to be an officer. Officers were higher-ranking, and usually a college education was enough to be eligible, but Jackie's application was denied. Joe Louis made a call on

his behalf, and the decision was reversed. Jackie did thirteen weeks of training and was promoted to second lieutenant.

Although hundreds of thousands of black Americans had volunteered or been drafted into military service, they lived and worked in segregated units. It wasn't clear whether the black units would ever be called into action. Jackie's unit spent two years waiting.

> The US military was finally desegregated in 1948, over a year after Major League Baseball.

A lot of people recognized Jackie as a football star from UCLA. Another officer asked him to play on the army's football team. But Jackie found out that he couldn't play in the first game, against an all-white college, because the college team didn't want to play against a black man. Jackie quit the army team.

He wasn't even allowed to try out for the baseball team. When he asked if he could, somebody told him to try out for the black team. There wasn't one.

Jackie's military career almost ended in disgrace. His battalion had been sent to Camp Hood, in Texas, where Jim Crow laws were strict. On a military bus, Jackie started talking to a friend—a light-skinned black woman. The driver insisted Jackie move to the back. Jackie refused. Though they were in the South, where laws ordered black people to ride in the back, Jackie knew the law didn't apply to military buses.

Refusing to Take a Back Seat

Jackie's refusal to change seats foreshadowed one of the central battles of the civil rights movement 10 years later.

March 2, 1955: Claudette Colvin, a black teenager in Montgomery, Alabama, refused to give up her seat on a city bus. Though less famous than Rosa Parks, Colvin's case went to the US Supreme Court and ended segregation of public transportation.

December 1, 1955: Rosa Parks, also of Montgomery, refused to give up her seat on a bus. Her arrest led to the Montgomery Bus Boycott, which received national attention. She was dubbed "the first lady of civil rights."

Jackie was especially angry after the driver called him a racist name. The driver contacted the military police. Jackie grew even angrier when the superior officer listened to every white person's side of the story before he would let Jackie talk. Finally, the officer placed Jackie under house arrest; that meant he could return to his barracks but would stand trial. It was a repeat of his experiences in Pasadena, where he'd been arrested three times for minor incidents.

Jackie was not officially in trouble for refusing to change seats. He was charged with disrespecting and disobeying a superior officer. Eight of the nine jurors were white, and only six were needed to convict him. Jackie explained his actions. The jury found him not guilty, but that was the end of Jackie's military career. He was released with an honorable discharge, officially for "physical disqualification," a strange explanation for kicking one of the best athletes in the country out of the army. The truth was probably that the army didn't want "troublemakers" like Second Lieutenant Jackie Robinson.

THE US ARMY'S "BLACK PANTHERS"

Jackie's tank battalion was sent to Europe while he waited for his trial. The 761st was the first African American tank battalion to see combat. It was also one of the most effective and decorated battalions in the war.

COME OUT FIGHTING

Jackie had broken up with Rachel while he was in the army. He was upset when she signed up to be an army nurse, thinking she would be leaving California. In fact, she was stationed in San Francisco. As soon as he got home, Jackie took the six-hour drive from Pasadena so he could apologize and make up. She had returned his engagement ring in the mail, but when he offered it back, she accepted. They decided they still wanted to get married. They didn't set a date, because the future was too much of an unknown.

CHAPTER 4

CHANGE COMES TO BASEBALL

Jackie was out of college and out of the army, but he didn't know what to do next. He didn't want just any job. He wanted to do something meaningful. He also wanted a good salary so he could raise a family. What could a black man do—especially one without a college degree?

In the army, Jackie had once noticed a black soldier named Ted Alexander throwing a ball around on a baseball field. Ted could throw a great curveball, and Jackie asked him where he'd learned how. Ted told him he'd pitched for the Kansas City Monarchs in the Negro Leagues. The black baseball teams needed good players, Ted said, because so many men had enlisted. The money wasn't on par with white baseball salaries, but it was better than most jobs open to black men. Jackie wrote a letter to the Monarchs, and they encouraged him to try out for the team in the spring. Jackie still hated segregation and second-class citizenship, but the Monarchs would pay him well. In the spring he tried out for the Monarchs. He easily made the team.

A Stormy Spring

Jackie's first few weeks with the Monarchs in 1945 were some of the most turbulent in world history.

April 12: President Franklin Delano Roosevelt dies of a stroke. Vice President Harry Truman is sworn in as president.

April 30: As the German military effort fails, and public support collapses, Adolf Hitler commits suicide, hastening the end of the war in Europe.

May 8: The war in Europe officially ends. The war in the Pacific continues through the summer.

Jackie quickly got a reputation as one of the best shortstops in the Negro Leagues, and he set records for on-base percentage and stolen bases. However, he was unhappy during his year with the Monarchs. He hated the Jim Crow laws of the South, where many public places wouldn't let him eat, sleep, or even go to the bathroom. He was frustrated that his teammates accepted the unfairness. Most of them had grown up in the South and didn't challenge the rules they'd always lived with. Jackie wanted to stand up for himself, as he had in California and in the army. When a service station owner refused to let the players use the bathroom, Jackie said they would buy their gas elsewhere. The owner quickly changed his mind.

Jackie, a disciplined player, was also frustrated by the casual style of the Negro Leagues. Games would begin late, or would end before the final inning if it was growing dark. The umpiring was sloppy. Life on the road was hard, too. Sometimes the team drove all day to play a night game, and drove on to the next city after the game. Most of all, Jackie missed Rachel. Now that she was back in his life, he didn't want to lose her again.

There were rumors that a black player might soon be signed to the major leagues, and Jackie must have known that his name was being tossed around as a possibility. But the player most people thought would be first was Jackie's teammate Leroy "Satchel" Paige. "Satch" was the biggest star in the Negro Leagues, and one of baseball's all-time greatest pitchers and personalities. He was so well known, his name was printed bigger than the names of either team on flyers advertising the games. He was a player famous for his many trick pitches. He gave some names, like the "Midnight Creeper," the "Whipsy-Dipsy-Do," and the "Hesitation Pitch." But even without trick pitches, Paige had a good fastball and the ability to keep throwing late into the game.

Age is a case of mind over matter. If you don't mind, it don't matter.

He had pitched against the best white hitters in exhibition games, and many of those players said he was the best pitcher they'd ever faced.

Paige deserved to be in the major leagues, but he was old for a pro athlete. Nobody knew exactly how old he was—the mystery was part of his legend—but he'd already been pitching for twenty years.

SATCHEL PAIGE
Pitcher

SATCHEL PAIGE

- Signed with the Cleveland Indians a year after Jackie's debut with the Dodgers and played for six seasons
- Still the oldest major-league rookie, starting at age 42, and the oldest player to appear in a major-league game, at age 58
- Led the Indians to a World Series victory in 1948
- Was never charged with a single error while in the major leagues
- Inducted into the Baseball Hall of Fame in 1971

In August of 1945, the Monarchs played a game in Chicago. After the game, a man walked up to Jackie. His name was Clyde Sukeforth, and he worked for the Brooklyn Dodgers. He told Jackie that Branch Rickey was starting his own Negro League team and was interested in signing Jackie to the team. Jackie was skeptical but agreed to go to New York.

"There's no new Negro League team," Rickey told Jackie as soon as he was in his office.

"I want you to play for the Montreal Royals next year. If that works out, you can play in Brooklyn the year after that."

Jackie was flabbergasted.

"You want me to play for the Dodgers?"

"That's right, but it won't be easy." Rickey didn't sugarcoat the offer. He let Jackie know how much abuse he would face. He even acted out some of the parts—prejudiced umpires, racist hotel and restaurant owners, and angry white ballplayers— yelling in Jackie's face to see how he would react.

Branch Rickey knew Jackie had been in trouble in the past, but he knew it was because Jackie was proud and had a strong will. He would need both if he was going to play Major League Baseball.

But now Jackie would have to "turn the other cheek," Rickey told him.

Are you looking for someone with the courage to fight back?

I'm looking for someone with the courage not to fight back.

He meant that Jackie couldn't fight back or even complain. Could he do it?

Jackie thought about his future with Rachel. He thought about his mother, who had worked so hard to raise her family. The money would make a big difference. But he was also won over by Branch Rickey's attitude.

"I'll do it," Jackie said.

His contract was big news! Many white sportswriters dismissed it as a publicity stunt and said he would never be good enough to play in the big leagues. Even people who were happy that a black player had made the team were disappointed that fan-favorite Satchel Paige hadn't been chosen. But Satchel Paige himself showed no bitterness.

"They couldn't have picked
a better man."
—Satchel Paige

⋚ AN UNHAPPY HONEYMOON ⋚

Jackie and Rachel were married on February 10, 1946, in Pasadena. A few weeks later, they set out for Daytona Beach, Florida, for spring training. Usually, wives were not allowed at training camp, but Branch Rickey had made an exception for Rachel because she and Jackie were newlyweds and because Rickey knew Jackie would need his wife's support. Jackie and Rachel had been separated for so much of the last five years, they were happy to finally have some time together.

Baseball Basics:
Spring Training

Since the 1900s, Major League Baseball teams have gathered in March to get ready for the season and play practice games. They now gather in Arizona and Florida, though historically they have had camps in other warm-weather regions.

More players are invited than can make the teams. Spring training is when managers decide their final rosters. For young players, it's an opportunity to show what they can do. For veteran players, it is often their last chance to prove they still have something to offer the team.

The Robinsons had trouble before they even got there. When they changed planes in New Orleans, the airline bumped them from the next flight, and then from one after that. White passengers were given their seats on both flights. Jackie and Rachel were very hungry, but none of the restaurants at the airport served black customers. Fortunately, Mallie had packed a meal for them. Rachel had been embarrassed by the box of cold chicken her new mother-in-law had forced on her at the airport in California, but now she understood why Mallie had insisted she take it.

As their wait dragged on, the airport officials suggested they get a hotel room and wait. But in New Orleans, a city that strongly supported Jim Crow, it was hard for a black couple to find a hotel room. They took a cab to a shabby, unclean room and waited for another several hours.

That night they were finally allowed to fly as far as Pensacola, Florida, but were once again bumped from their flight to Daytona. There were no hotels in Pensacola that took black guests. Jackie and Rachel boarded a bus for an exhausting sixteen-hour trip. They were not even allowed to sit in the next-to-last seats, which reclined, but were forced to sit in the very back row.

Jackie, who had refused to change seats while in the army, now had to swallow his rage.

They arrived in Daytona a day late, tired and annoyed. The hotel where the white players stayed refused to give the Robinsons a room, so they rented a room in the house of a local black businessman. They had just a bedroom and had to eat all their meals at cheap restaurants.

Jackie was not the only black player at training camp. There was also John Wright, a pitcher Jackie had met in the Negro Leagues. Most of the white players were cold to Jackie and John. They knew they'd be in big trouble if they picked fights with the two black men or called them names, so instead the whites largely ignored them.

Jackie faced taunting and abuse as the team traveled to play other teams in spring-training games. In one game, Jackie was not allowed to take the field because local law banned integrated sports. A sheriff appeared in the middle of another game and ordered Jackie and John to leave. In yet another, the game was canceled because the lights weren't working—even though it was a day game, in the famous Florida sunshine.

One night on the road, Jackie, Rachel, and John Wright were hurried out of town. A hostile white mob had gathered and was heading toward the house where they were all staying.

The hardship got to Jackie, and he started making mistakes on the field and swinging at bad pitches. He tried to make up for it by playing extra hard, but ended up hurting his arm. He played even worse. Reporters began to write that Mr. Rickey's noble experiment was a failure. His teammates began to wonder if Jackie's presence was worth the trouble.

Jackie didn't have a good spring training, but Branch Rickey didn't give up on him. Jackie still made the Montreal Royals, the Dodgers' Triple-A affiliate.

Baseball Basics: Organized Baseball

Most professional baseball teams throughout the United States, Canada, Mexico, and the Dominican Republic are affiliated with major-league teams. Minor-league teams allow players to develop and prepare to play in the majors. There are several levels. Each major-league team has one or more teams at each level, like rungs on a ladder, for the players to ascend before reaching the top. Players may skip a rung or two but rarely go straight to the major leagues without a stint in the minors.

The succesion of levels (from top to bottom) are:

- **Major League**
  - **Triple-A**
  - **Double-A**
  - **Class A**
- **Rookie League**

Only about one player in 10 in the minor leagues makes it to the major leagues.

Jackie's playing took a sharp turn for the better even before he got to Canada. The Royals had a few games on the road before their first home game. Jackie had stellar games in Baltimore, Maryland, and in Jersey City, New Jersey. His new teammates started treating him better. Color didn't matter so much, he discovered, when you were a winner.

Jackie had two things going for him that made the turnaround possible.

The first was black fans coming out to the ballpark to cheer for him.

They're all counting on me. I can't let them down.

The second was Rachel. Their young marriage grew strong as they leaned on each other to get through the slump and the hardship of the Jim Crow South. However, Rachel realized by the end of that spring, it wouldn't be just the two of them for long. There would be three Robinsons by the end of the year.

CHAPTER 5

THE LONELIEST MAN IN SPORTS

Montreal, in Quebec, Canada, could not have been more different from Daytona for the Robinsons. The Montreal Royals fans loved Jackie, and their new neighbors welcomed them. The women made a fuss over Rachel when they learned she was pregnant.

The local fans were good to Jackie, but people on the road were far less friendly. In Baltimore, a restless mob surrounded the visitors' locker room and yelled for his teammates to send Jackie out. The police didn't come, so the Royals had to wait for the crowd to give up and go home. In Syracuse, players threw a black cat out of the dugout. "There's your cousin, Jackie!" they taunted. Everywhere the Royals went, white fans yelled racial slurs at Jackie.

Jackie kept his promise to Branch Rickey and didn't lose his temper, but that didn't mean the abuse never got to him. Inside, he was troubled. He ate poorly and slept poorly. Rachel said he seemed to be coming apart at the seams.

Yet he continued to play well, funneling his frustration into aggressive base running and solid hitting. His black teammate, John Wright, could not take the pressure. He played poorly and was cut from the team. Jackie now had to bear the weight alone. He was the first black ballplayer to play against all-white teams up and down the East Coast. Somehow, he managed to get through the season, thanks to the love of Rachel, the support of black fans at every stadium, and the warm acceptance of the people in Montreal.

In fact, he not only got through the season but led the league in scoring.

Behind Jackie, the Royals won a hundred games, placing first in their league. The final test came in Kentucky, where they faced the Louisville Colonels in the Junior World Series. Louisville fans made it one of the most hostile places Jackie would ever play. He went into a short slump, and Montreal dropped two of three games. A scout sent a worried note to Branch Rickey that Robinson might not be able to handle the pressure of the cities in the South where the Dodgers played.

The tables turned in Montreal. Royals fans, having read about how Robinson was treated in Louisville, showered the Colonels with taunts and boos of their own. The Royals won all the games there and took the series. In the final game, it was Jackie who scored the winning run! He was swarmed by fans on the field. He even had trouble going home—his fans followed him and ripped the clothes on his back!

Jackie did not know until later that Royals manager Clay Hopper resented Rickey's experiment. Hopper was a Southerner and a segregationist. He had once asked Rickey—in all sincerity—if he considered black people to be human. To his credit, Hopper kept his uglier feelings to himself and behaved professionally. He managed Robinson fairly and treated him well. In the end, Robinson's skill and class on the field made Hopper a convert.

"He's a player who must go to the majors. He's a big-league player."
—Clay Hopper

Nobody could doubt that Jackie had earned a spot with the Dodgers, but Rickey hadn't made it official yet. The Robinsons returned to California to await the birth of their baby and news from Brooklyn.

⋲ CALLED UP ⋲

In fact, Jackie still didn't know his fate when he boarded a plane for Havana, Cuba, in February 1947. He also didn't know that at a meeting the month before, the major-league team owners had voted, 15–1, in favor of an official rule against integration. Branch Rickey was the sole vote against it. The commissioner of baseball, Happy Chandler, disallowed the vote, so Rickey's plan was still on course. But Rickey knew how deep the opposition to the plan went.

There were now four black players in the Dodgers organization, including Robinson, catcher Roy Campanella, and pitchers Don Newcombe and Roy Partlow. Rickey decided to spend spring training in Cuba for that reason. Cuba's population was mostly mixed-race, and the baseball teams there were already integrated. Rickey hoped to avoid the kinds of trouble the team had experienced in Florida.

It was a rough month for Jackie, who was sick most of the time—unused to the food and water—and who found Jim Crow–like conditions in some of the places they played. He missed Rachel and his three-month-old son, Jackie Jr., terribly. As he had done in the past, Jackie was able to ignore all the tough things going on in his personal life and play brilliantly.

When it became clear that Jackie was playing well enough to make the team, some of the Dodgers complained. Dixie Walker, a star outfielder for the Dodgers, was suspected of circulating a petition among the white players, stating they would not play if Robinson did. Walker later claimed there was never a petition, but he did not deny that the Southern white players objected to Jackie's promotion and that Walker was their ringleader. Manager Leo Durocher roused the players in the middle of the night. He told them anyone who didn't want to play with Robinson would get traded or cut.

"I don't care if he's black or yellow or has stripes like a zebra! I'm the manager, and I say he plays."
—Leo Durocher

The Royals and Dodgers finished their spring training with two exhibition games at Ebbets Field in Brooklyn. Robinson played in both games as a Royal before huge crowds of black fans. In the middle of the second game, Rickey's assistant brought a handful of hastily typed press releases and handed them out to the reporters.

```
The Brooklyn Dodgers today
purchased the contract of
Jackie Roosevelt Robinson
from the Montreal Royals.
He will report immediately.

Very truly yours,
```

Branch Rickey

```
Branch Rickey,
President.


        [End of press release]
```

⌇ A LONELY DECISION ⌇

And then it happened! On April 15, 1947, Jackie was a Dodger. Some people though Rickey might take it slow, putting Jackie in as a pinch runner late in the game, but Jackie was in the starting lineup and batted second.

Here we are back at that historic moment with Jackie coming to the plate, grounding out to third, and not picking a fight with the umpire. Many fans cheered as if he'd hit a grand-slam home run, because they knew what a big moment it was for baseball and for history. The day is memorialized as the day the color line was crossed and segregated baseball ended—but it didn't happen in a day. In truth, Jackie Robinson brought integration to the majors slowly, one ballpark at a time, and one opponent at a time.

The next big test came a few days into the season, at Ebbets Field, in a game against the Philadelphia Phillies. As he went to bat in the first inning, Jackie heard the Phillies harassing him from the dugout. They called him the worst racist names and made awful jokes, trying to make Jackie feel ashamed of his uniform and his own skin.

The ugliness continued all day, encouraged by
the Phillies' own manager, a former player named
Ben Chapman. Chapman was well known for his bad
attitude and prejudice. In the lead-up to World War II,
he'd taunted Jewish fans and players with Nazi salutes.
He hurled insults at players whose names were Italian
or Polish. But this was the worst he'd ever been.

Jackie bubbled with anger. He imagined throwing his bat, storming into the dugout, and punching Chapman's face. But what had it all been for—standing up for himself in college, getting into trouble in the army—if he was going to give it all away now by flying off the handle at this petty man?

It was not thoughts of himself, his wife or mother, or even his baby that made Jackie hold his anger. It was Branch Rickey. He knew Rickey had made "a lonely decision," and now Jackie would make his own. He kept his cool.

The abuse continued all afternoon. Late in the game, Dodgers second baseman Eddie Stanky had heard enough. He stormed over to the Phillies dugout.

Listen, you yellow-bellied cowards! Why don't you yell at someone who can answer back?

It was a turning point with the team, as the rest of the Dodgers came around to accept Jackie as a teammate. But he was still kept at arm's length off the field. He was never included in the friendly chatter in the locker room. Rachel, who brought baby Jackie Jr. to home games, was not greeted by the other players' wives.

Jackie went into a slump, going several games without a hit and making mistakes on the field. He was trying to get used to major-league pitching and learn a new fielding position—first base. Those are tall challenges for any rookie, and Jackie was playing under a lot of pressure! The world was watching his every move, and many were hoping he would fail. The crowds were calling out things that were far more mean-spirited than the usual taunts. And his own teammates, though polite and respectful, were distant.

"He is the loneliest man
I have ever seen in sports."
—Jimmy Cannon, *New York Post*

Jackie was forced to "make up" with Chapman when the Dodgers went to Philadelphia a few weeks later. The two men posed and smiled for the camera, and immediately afterward Chapman muttered a few more slurs. Once the game was on, the childish name-calling from the Phillies dugout continued. Chapman didn't take part, but he may have encouraged it, and sure didn't use his position as manager to stop it.

Later that month the Dodgers played the Cardinals in St. Louis. A newspaper broke the story that the Cardinals were planning to strike and hoped other teams would do the same. The newspaper reported that Ford Frick, the president of the National League (see page 104), responded quickly: any player attempting to strike, he said, would be suspended. If they had to suspend half the players in the league, so be it.

> "The National League will go down the line with Robinson, whatever the consequence."
> —Ford Frick

Sports reporters wrote about Chapman's abuse and the rumors of a Cardinals strike but didn't really comment on Jackie's day-to-day challenges. In every opponent's ballpark, fans yelled racist words at him. Opponents and workers at the ballparks muttered insults under their breath. Sometimes, when Jackie was nearby, his own teammates would tell racist jokes to see if they could get a rise out of him.

Even in Northern cities, hotels or restaurants would refuse him service. Sometimes he found another place to eat or spend the night. Other times, the entire team switched, and his fellow players would grumble that they had to settle for second class.

Mr. Rickey told me that when my teammates began to rally to my cause, we could consider the battle half won.

Every day, Jackie received hate mail and threats. The anonymous letter-writers said they'd kill Jackie if he stepped foot in their hometown ballpark. Some even threatened Rachel and Jackie Jr. Jackie thought the letter writers were cowards who would never act on their threats, but Branch Rickey passed the letters on to the police. Nothing came of it. The insults and threats piled up. It started getting to Jackie, and he struggled at the plate and on the field. He had resisted the urge to throw his career away by punching Chapman in the face, but now his future was suffering "death by a thousand cuts."

DID YOU SEE JACKIE ROBINSON HIT THAT BALL?

But by June, Jackie started to get hits. He was once again able to channel his frustration into his sport. The Dodgers players started being a bit friendlier to him, too. Many fans, even those in opponents' ballparks, began to cheer for him. They had read about his mistreatment in the newspaper and wanted to let him know he had supporters, too. Branch Rickey traded away another first baseman, giving Jackie a jolt of confidence that he'd be there all season.

There's a legend about Dodgers shortstop Pee Wee Reese. He was originally against Jackie's presence on the team. In Cincinnati, the legend goes, people in the stands were abusing Jackie, as always. Pee Wee was from nearby Louisville and had a lot of friends, family, and fans who were there to root for him. According to the story, Reese walked across the infield and threw an arm around Jackie to show the fans that he supported him. It quieted the crowd. The moment is so famous that there is a statue outside a minor-league ballpark in Brooklyn. There's even a picture book about it.

However, it probably never happened—at least not exactly like that. Just as Jackie didn't end the color line in one at-bat, one famous moment didn't end the racist treatment Jackie experienced. It is true, though, that Pee Wee and Jackie became friends, and Pee Wee was more likely than the other players to chat with him in the locker room or slap hands after a run was scored.

CHAPTER 6

A WORLD SERIES VICTORY

By the middle of his first season, Jackie was no longer just a symbol. He was a genuine superstar! His biggest impact was on the lives of black children. Whether or not they wanted to be baseball players, they saw possibilities for their own futures while watching Jackie. Every day he received letters from children all over America about the hope he'd given them.

Jackie's appeal crossed color lines. Author Myron Uhlberg wrote of how his deaf father connected with Jackie because they were both out of place in the world. Bette Bao Lord wrote a fictionalized memoir called *In the Year of the Boar and Jackie Robinson*, about how Jackie's courage helped her overcome her own barriers as a Chinese immigrant. Anyone who had ever been told they didn't belong, or who stood out for their differences, felt a connection.

And some fans loved Jackie simply because he was an exciting player to watch. He would get on base, take a lead, and dare the pitcher to make a throw. He was always a threat to steal. He would steal third base with two outs. He would steal home! Some fans compared him to baseball's all-time greatest base runner, Ty Cobb. Jackie's fearlessness on the base path lifted the rest of the team. They hit better because the pitchers were rattled and infielders were distracted.

Memorabilia

- Buddy Johnson record, "Did You See Jackie Robinson Hit That Ball?"

- Collectible cards

- Cover of *Time* magazine

- Jackie Robinson comic book

Baseball Basics:
Pennants and Playoffs

Major League Baseball has two leagues that arose separately: the National League and the American League. Since 1916, the two teams who win their respective leagues go on to play in the World Series for the championship. The first team to win four games wins the World Series.

Until 1969, a team would win its league simply by having the best record. A playoff game or series was necessary only if two teams tied, which rarely happened. When two teams were close in the standings, vying for the best record, it was called a "pennant race," named for the flag the victorious team could fly at their home ballpark.

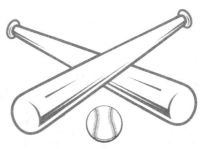

In July, the Cleveland Indians signed Larry Doby, a Negro League star. They brought him directly to Cleveland to play, letting him skip the minor leagues. Since American League teams didn't face National League teams during the regular season, Doby was the first black player in most American League ballparks and faced many of the same challenges Jackie did.

The St. Louis Browns, in last place in the American League, then signed two black players, Willard Brown and Hank Thompson. The Browns became the first team to play two black players in the same game. Unfortunately, the historic event didn't draw huge crowds of supporters the way Jackie did in Brooklyn, probably because the Browns were the worst team in the major leagues. By August, there was another black player on the Dodgers, pitcher Dan Bankhead. Jackie Robinson was no longer the only black man in Major League Baseball, and he didn't have to bear the pressure of representing all black players. He could just be Jackie Robinson.

By the end of the season, Jackie had proved he was one of the best players in the game, especially in base running. The Dodgers won first place in the National League. They lost the World Series to the New York Yankees, but nobody could deny that Branch Rickey's experiment was a smashing success.

Jackie with the Brooklyn Dodgers
1947

→ Jackie leads the league in stolen bases, with 29.

→ Jackie is second in the league for runs scored, with 125.

→ Jackie finishes in the top 20 in the league for batting average (.297) and on-base percentage (.383).

→ Jackie leads the Dodgers in hits, with 175.

→ Jackie wins the first-ever Rookie of the Year Award.

⋛ JUST ANOTHER GUY ⋚

The following season, former Negro League star Roy
Campanella came up to the Dodgers, and Satchel
Paige joined the Indians. The St. Louis Browns cut their
two black players when they didn't bring hordes of new
fans to games, as the owner had hoped. One of those
players, Hank Thompson, would sign with the Giants
and have the historic distinction of being the first black
player to have played on two different teams.

Jackie was not the only black major-league
player anymore, or even the only one in the
Dodgers infield.

He moved to second base, where he would stay for
most of his career. He still took abuse, but he began to
see changes. His own teammates warmed up to him.
In fact, he became the center of the team's identity.
They now took pride in being the first integrated and
the most integrated team in baseball. Jackie was able
to be himself, and that meant being more outspoken!

In one game he was ejected for complaining to an
umpire. He was delighted. He wasn't ejected for being
black; he was ejected for complaining—as any player
could be.

One headline summed it up perfectly:

★ EXTRA! ★

JACKIE
JUST ANOTHER GUY

Late in his second season, Jackie was called into Branch Rickey's office. Rickey told Jackie he no longer needed to "turn the other cheek." He could stand up for himself.

Jackie, you're on your own now. You can be yourself now.

Jackie Robinson enjoyed his new freedom right away. At spring training in 1949, he challenged a pitcher to a fight after the pitcher threw a "beanball"—a pitch at a batter's head. He also started arguing more with the umpires. Jackie said he wanted the umpires to be fair. He felt they were often biased against him.

He wasn't afraid to share his opinions with Dodgers coaches, either. Jackie had been forced to be silent for so long; now everything gushed out, one teammate said. The newspapers painted Jackie as a troublemaker. But he was also judged more harshly than were white players who argued with umpires and coaches.

"He was a holler guy— but that was part of his being a Dodger." —Carl Erskine, Dodgers pitcher

Jackie could finally speak his mind and he wasn't worried about the effect it might have on his reputation. He thought his outspokenness even helped the Dodgers grow closer as a team, since many of his comments were in defense of the other players.

One sportswriter who had always supported Jackie confronted him about his new behavior.

In 1949, Jackie had his best season—he played in more games, had more hits, batted in more runs, and stole more bases than he did in any other season.

I don't care if anyone likes me as long as they respect me.

Jackie, you know the sports reporters vote on all the awards. No matter how well you play, they won't vote for you if they don't like you.

He won the award for Most Valuable Player, which was voted on by the very sportswriters he had been sparring with all season.

★ THE ★
MOST
VALUABLE
PLAYER

"The Bums"

In 1947, 1949, 1952, and 1953, the Dodgers won the pennant, or league championship, just to lose the World Series to their cross-town rivals, the New York Yankees. The Dodgers were nicknamed "the Bums" because they'd lost so many World Series. But Dodgers fans were faithful. "Next year!" was their rallying cry every time the Dodgers lost.

However, the Dodgers' most famous postseason defeat came against the Giants in 1951. The Dodgers headed into August with a big lead, just to watch it crumble as the Giants went on a tear, and the Dodgers went into a slump. The two teams finished the season in a tie, prompting a three-game playoff. Each won a game, then held a tiebreaker at the Polo Grounds, the Giants' home stadium. The Dodgers took a lead into the bottom of the ninth, but Bobby Thomson of the Giants hit a line-drive home run, scoring three runs and winning the game. The "shot heard around the world" became one of the most famous moments in baseball history.

While the rest of the Dodgers slunk off the field, Robinson, a competitor to the end, watched Thomson circle the bases, hoping he would miss one and be out on a technicality. No such luck.

The Giants went on to lose the World Series to the Yankees. Even if Dodgers outfielder Andy Pafko had managed to catch Thomson's line drive, and the Dodgers had won the pennant, the Yankees probably would have won anyway. After all, the Yankees had beaten the Dodgers in 1947 and 1949. They would do it again in 1952 and 1953.

Going into the 1954 season, Jackie Robinson had deeper reasons for resenting the Yankees than frustrating losses. By that year, four teams had still failed to sign a black player; the Yankees were one of them. Jackie had made the full integration of baseball a personal goal. He was outspoken about it on the field and off. He criticized Yankees manager Casey Stengel, who was known to freely use racial slurs. On a TV program in 1952, Jackie was asked if he felt the Yankees remained an all-white team because of bigotry. He answered bluntly that he did.

The Dodgers now featured four black players, including Jackie, catcher Roy Campanella, and pitchers Don Newcombe and Joe Black. The Giants had Monte Irvin, Hank Thompson, and Willie Mays. The Cubs had Ernie Banks. The Braves, who had moved from Boston to Milwaukee, had a promising rookie named Henry "Hank" Aaron. It was the "first generation of black superstars," as sportswriter Bill Madden called it. "Hammerin' Hank" went on to set most of major-league baseball's career hitting records and still holds three. He is now in the Hall of Fame, as are Ernie Banks, Ray Campanella, and Willie Mays.

WILLIE MAYS

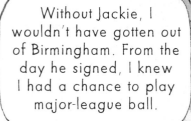

Without Jackie, I wouldn't have gotten out of Birmingham. From the day he signed, I knew I had a chance to play major-league ball.

HANK AARON

He was my hero and always has been. Not only for the baseball that he played, but simply because of the person he was.

Most of baseball at that time was integrated, but a few teams seemed to be fighting it to the last breath. While emerging black stars like Willie Mays didn't want to rock the boat, Jackie Robinson wasn't afraid to lift his voice about the bigotry that still existed in baseball. He was criticized in the newspapers, called a rabble-rouser and a troublemaker.

Jackie responded that if the Yankees wanted to prove they weren't racists, all they had to do was sign a black player. At one point he was called into the commissioner's office. Robinson went, sure he'd be disciplined or fined. Commissioner Frick told him that he had to hear both sides because of his job, but he supported Jackie.

Between you and me, you're right and they're wrong.

The following year, the Yankees brought up Elston Howard, their first black player.

WHEN "NEXT YEAR" FINALLY CAME

Jackie also butted heads with his own team leadership. In 1950, the other owners had forced out Branch Rickey, whom Jackie loved like a father. The new team president was Walter O'Malley, who called Jackie a "prima donna," meaning someone who thinks a lot of themself! The two men never got along. In 1954, the team manager was Walter Alston. Alston was quiet and low-key, unlikely to take sides when Jackie had it out with umpires.

As a veteran, Jackie embraced his role as a mentor to younger Dodgers, white or black. In 1955, the Dodgers signed a rookie pitcher from Brooklyn. After a couple of disastrous outings, the young pitcher was benched for weeks. His contract said that he couldn't be sent to the minor leagues, so he sat in the bullpen. Robinson argued with Alston, saying the kid had talent and needed more chances to prove himself. Finally, late in the season, the rookie got another chance to play and pitched two shutout games. Though he would struggle for a few more seasons before mastering the game, Sandy Koufax would go on to be the best pitcher of his era.

He and Jackie were voted number one and number two respectively in a poll among fans of the greatest Dodgers of all time.

Even with several players grumbling about Alston's management, the Dodgers had a great season. They won their first ten games and never looked back. They won the pennant and then took a collective deep breath as they prepared once again to face their old rivals, the New York Yankees.

Jackie played a variety of positions that season, mostly third base and right field, to make room for Jim Gilliam, the Dodgers' new up-and-coming second baseman. Jackie didn't play in as many games as he used to, because he wasn't playing as well. But he made the best-known play of that World Series, and probably the most famous play in his career. In the eighth inning of the first game, with the Dodgers trailing by two runs, Jackie Robinson was on third base with a pinch hitter at the plate.

Catching for the Yankees was Lawrence "Yogi" Berra. Jackie had tested Yogi since they were both rookies in the 1947 World Series. He did it again, sprinting for home with a pitch. Berra caught the ball and moved to block the plate and apply the tag. Jackie slid under the tag and touched the plate with his toe.

Berra, normally known for his good humor, threw off his mask and yelled at the umpire while Jackie trotted back to the dugout. The Dodgers lost that game, but the play gave them a jolt of confidence they needed. They went on to win the series in seven games. The Dodgers—who had lost the first World Series and had lost more World Series than any other team—had finally won a championship.

CHAPTER 7

LIFE AFTER BASEBALL

Jackie's tenth and final season was uneven. He displayed flashes of his former brilliance but was also showing his age. He did not yet know that he had diabetes, which was taking its toll. He was at his best toward the end of the season, in a pennant race with the Giants. "[Jackie] is still the most dangerous individual in the game," one sportswriter wrote. The Dodgers won the pennant but lost yet another World Series to the Yankees.

Between 1921 and 1956, 13 World Series were played between New York teams: seven between the Yankees and Dodgers, six between the Yankees and Giants.

Jackie planned on coming back in 1957. At the last minute, the Dodgers traded him to the Giants. Jackie decided to retire instead. He'd suffered more than his share of insults as a player. To be traded to the Dodgers' archrival was one insult too many.

Ironically, a year later, the Dodgers moved to Los Angeles, where Jackie had first emerged as a national star. The team's new home was ten miles from Pasadena, where Jackie had grown up and where his mother and siblings still lived. If his health had held up long enough for him to play there, it would have been a movie-perfect final act to his career.

However, Jackie already had a very different vision for his coming years. Chock Full o'Nuts, the biggest chain of coffee shops in the northeastern United States, had offered him a position. As vice president, Jackie became the first black executive of a major corporation. The company founder felt Jackie's reputation would help him manage their employees, most of whom were black.

In some ways, this was more groundbreaking, if less storied, than Jackie's debut with the Dodgers. Sports and entertainment were open to talented black people, but business was still very much a white man's world. Jackie didn't want to be merely a figurehead.

He related to the staff well, many of whom were trying to raise families on modest wages, because of his own childhood. But the job brought new challenges.

This is harder than baseball ever was.

In the last years of his baseball career, Jackie used his fame and reputation to pressure hotels and restaurants in the South into serving him and giving him service equal to that of the white clientele.

He wanted to go to the best restaurants and hotels, of course, but he also wanted to use his celebrity to force change. He knew if they served him, it would be that much easier for the next black customer to get served.

Other Firsts

Jackie Robinson was a pioneer in many things related to sports, and he went on to break new ground after his retirement, too. He was the first:

- black executive at a major company (Chock Full o'Nuts)
- black nationally syndicated newspaper columnist for a white-owned paper (the *New York Post*)
- regular black broadcaster on a major network (ABC's Major League Baseball Game of the Week)

Meanwhile, the civil rights movement was taking shape in the South, particularly in Montgomery, Alabama. Robinson, who had once been arrested after refusing to give up his bus seat, followed the Rosa Parks story with great interest. At that time he was still playing, and so he could not be more involved, but he admired the leader who emerged in Montgomery: the Reverend Martin Luther King Jr. King was a believer in nonviolent resistance, bringing change through protest and other peaceful methods.

He's the best leader we have, maybe the best we ever had.

Once he was out of baseball, Jackie was eager to do more for civil rights. The National Association for the Advancement of Colored People (NAACP) asked Jackie to head up their Freedom Fund Drive. For the next year, Jackie would travel around the country to give speeches and host fund-raising dinners to raise money that helped pay legal fees for the men and women who were leading protests fighting to end segregation. He wrote to Martin Luther King Jr., encouraging him to join the ambitious fund drive. King agreed, and the two men became friends over the next year.

SEGREGATED SCHOOLS

The issue that inspired Jackie the most was school integration. The US Supreme Court had ruled in 1954 that segregated schools were unconstitutional, but leaders in the Southern states resisted the new law. In 1957, the governor of Arkansas blockaded the entrance to Little Rock High School to stop black students from entering. The story in Little Rock outraged the nation, and Jackie Robinson especially.

"I tried to see a friendly face in the crowd—someone who maybe could help. I looked into the face of an old woman and it seemed a kind face, but when I looked at her again, she spat on me."
—Elizabeth Eckford, Little Rock student

Many people urged President Dwight D. Eisenhower to send in troops to escort the black students safely to their classrooms. The president told them to be patient, that school integration would take time. Jackie wrote to Eisenhower, knowing his letter would rise to the top and be read by the president himself.

I respectfully remind you, sir, that we have been the most patient of all people. When you said we must have self-respect, I wondered how we could have self-respect and remain patient considering the treatment accorded us through the years.

Jackie Robinson

A few weeks later, when Eisenhower finally took action, Jackie wrote him a thank-you letter. He said:

"I should have known you would do the right thing at the crucial time."

A CALL FROM COOPERSTOWN

The National Baseball Hall of Fame and Museum is a baseball history center in Cooperstown, New York. The highest honor for a baseball player is to be included in the Hall of Fame. As the first black major-league player, Jackie would likely be the first black Hall of Famer. But some argued that his baseball accomplishments didn't support Hall of Fame status, that he was a "good but not great" player.

Others argued that his achievements and importance went beyond statistics—that stats alone don't begin to tell the story of Jackie Robinson. Even the famous sportswriter Dick Young, who had been critical of Jackie for years, wrote that Jackie belonged in the Hall of Fame:

"Jackie Robinson made baseball history, and that's what the Hall of Fame is, baseball history."

When it came down to it, in his first year of eligibility, Jackie Robinson was voted in. At the ceremony, Jackie spoke humbly, thanking the Hall of Fame committee for giving him a platform to help others. He donated the proceeds of a dinner held in his honor to a prominent civil rights group. Martin Luther King Jr. wrote an article, "Hall of Famer," in celebration of Jackie Robinson's achievement.

"Back in the days when integration wasn't fashionable, he underwent the trauma and the humiliation and the loneliness which comes with being a pilgrim walking the lonesome byways toward the high road of Freedom."
—Martin Luther King Jr.

Measuring Greatness

In 1985, baseball analyst Bill James released a detailed book of historical baseball stats. In the book, James shows that Robinson was the best second baseman in baseball from 1949 through 1952, and the fourth best of all time, based on stats alone.

In 1963, King led a lengthy standoff with authorities in Birmingham, Alabama, the most segregated city in the United States. He was arrested.

Jackie held a jazz concert as a fund-raiser at his home in Connecticut to help pay the legal costs of King and other protesters. The concert became an annual event.

Later that year Jackie and his family joined King at the famous March on Washington, where King gave his "I Have a Dream" speech. It was August 28, 1963, the eighteenth anniversary of the day Jackie met Branch Rickey.

In 1964, Jackie helped to found Freedom National Bank in Harlem. His hope was that by helping people start businesses and buy homes, the bank could strengthen New York's largest black community. He also worked for the governor of New York, Nelson Rockefeller, as an assistant on community affairs. He was active in politics, campaigning for candidates he felt best understood and supported civil rights. He was independent, supporting Republicans in some races and Democrats in others.

Meanwhile, he and Rachel raised their family. His children were Jackie Jr., Sharon, and David. In his autobiography, Jackie writes about the challenges and rewards of parenting.

On October 15, 1972, Major League Baseball invited Jackie to throw out the ceremonial first pitch in the second game of the World Series. Jackie thanked the commissioner for the honor and took advantage of the moment to make his final plea for integration.

"I must admit I'm going to be . . . more proud when I look at that third-base coaching line one day and see a black face managing in baseball."
—Jackie Robinson

Three years later, Frank Robinson—no relation to Jackie—fulfilled that dream when he became manager of the Cleveland Indians. Unfortunately, Jackie would not live to see it happen. He had been diagnosed with diabetes shortly after he retired from baseball. Despite having fought many battles in public, he fought this one in private. He never talked about his illness in public. But people could see that his health was failing. He was going blind and walked with the gait of a much older man. On the morning of October 24, 1972, he died at home at the age of fifty-three.

CONCLUSION

A LEGACY

There is a saying that some are born great, some achieve greatness, and some have greatness thrust upon them. Jackie Robinson was certainly born great, with gifts that made him succeed in every sport he tried. He also had greatness thrust upon him by Branch Rickey. But the greatness Jackie Robinson seized and made for himself is the one that makes him the towering figure he is now. He knew his importance as a symbol and tried to do the most good he could with his celebrity.

"If I had a room jammed with trophies, awards, and citations, and a child of mine came to me in that room and asked what I had done in defense of black people and decent whites fighting for freedom—and I had to tell that child that I had been quiet, that I had been timid, I would have to mark myself a total failure in the whole business of living."

Over the years, Major League Baseball came to realize just how important Jackie was to the sport by ending its shameful history of segregation. In 1987, baseball's Rookie of the Year Award was renamed in honor of its first recipient, Jackie Robinson.

On April 15, 1997, the fiftieth anniversary of his debut with the Dodgers, Jackie's number, 42, became the first and only to be retired across all of organized baseball. Major-league and minor-league teams no longer use it.

One player who did where the number was Yankees pitcher Mariano "Mo" Rivera, who had grown up on the streets of Panama City and played ball with a homemade cardboard mitt. Mo had just been named the Yankees closer, the specialized role for a pitcher who protects a small lead in the final innings. Rivera went on to be the greatest closer there ever was. He was the last to wear the number 42 on an everyday basis and told reporters what an honor it was to wear it. He retired in 2013.

Since 2004, April 15 has been "Jackie Robinson Day." All players now wear number 42 for one day in celebration of Jackie and of the new era of baseball he brought.

BOOKS AND MOVIES

Jackie Robinson has been the subject of lots of films, stage plays, TV specials, books, and even comic books. Over five thousand books have been written about Jackie—more than have been written about Babe Ruth!

→ Jackie wrote four books at different stages in his career; the last is *I Never Had It Made*, released a few days after his death.

→ The children's novel *The Hero Two Doors Down* covers Jackie's early days with the Dodgers and was written by his daughter, Sharon Robinson. It's the best known of several books she's written about her father and her family.

→ Jackie played himself in the 1950 movie *The Jackie Robinson Story*.

→ Jackie was played by Chadwick Boseman in the 2013 movie *42*.

→ Filmmaker Ken Burns made a four-hour documentary about Jackie Robinson, with more attention to his personal life and politics than his baseball career.

Shortly after Jackie's death, Rachel Robinson founded the Jackie Robinson Foundation, an organization that gives scholarships and support to college students. In 2017, Rachel Robinson was inducted into the Baseball Hall of Fame when she received the Buck O'Neil Lifetime Achievement Award, given only once every three years to "an individual who enhances baseball's positive image on society, who broadens the game's appeal, and whose integrity and dignity are comparable to the namesake of the award." Jackie, who had been "the first" in so many ways, became so again forty-four years after his passing. He and Rachel became the first married couple who were both inducted into the Hall of Fame.

The Jackie Robinson Foundation's four-year program has supported 1,450 students from over 225 different colleges and universities across the country.

Who Is John "Buck" O'Neil?

- Played with the Kansas City Monarchs from 1937-1955 (served in the military during Robinson's year with the team)
- First black coach in Major League Baseball (Chicago Cubs, 1962)
- Helped to found the Negro Leagues Baseball Museum in Kansas City, 1990

"Jackie wasn't built the way we were. We were conditioned to segregation. We were conditioned to Jim Crow. We knew it wasn't right, but we saw it as unchangeable part of the world. Jackie didn't see it that way. Jackie knew the times would change. He would make them change."
—John "Buck" O'Neil

Across the country, various schools, Little League teams, parks, and baseball fields are named for Jackie Robinson. At UCLA, the athletic facilities are named for him. Outside the Rose Bowl stadium in Pasadena, where he once played football, is a statue. Across the street from City Hall in Pasadena is a memorial to both Jackie and his brother Mack. Outside the minor-league ballpark in Brooklyn is that statue of Jackie standing with Pee Wee Reese. In Georgia, ten miles south of Cairo, is a plaque noting the spot where Jackie was born—the house had burned down years before.

Jackie has been the subject of three US Postal Service stamps. They celebrate (in order) black heritage, most memorable moments of the 20th century, and all-time greatest baseball players.

These days, the name "Jackie Robinson" is often used for anyone who brings down barriers or is the first one who enters an area that wasn't previously open to people like them. The burden of being a "Jackie Robinson," many learn, means being twice as good and still facing more criticism.

For those reasons, nearly sixty-two years after Jackie Robinson stepped foot on Ebbets Field, former US President Barack Obama has been described as the ultimate Jackie Robinson: as the first black president, he inspired children of all races to believe what they could achieve, and he showed the same grace and courage as he weathered criticism that sometimes carried a racist tinge.

"There's a direct line between Jackie Robinson and me standing here." —Barack Obama

But Jackie Robinson worried that his own story would be used as a fairy tale.

"As one of those who has 'made it,' I would like to be thought of as an inspiration to our young," Jackie wrote in his autobiography. "But I don't want them lied to."

"I'm grateful for all the breaks and honors and opportunities I've had, but I always believe I won't have it made until the humblest black kid in the most remote backwoods of America has it made."
–Jackie Robinson

JACKIE ROBINSON

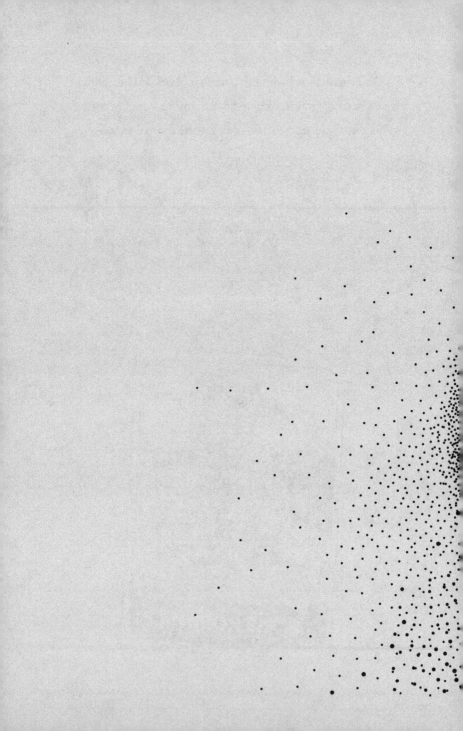

Timeline

August 5
Jackie's brother Mac
competes in the Olympi
in Berlin, winning
the silver medal in
the 200-meter dash.

January 31
Jackie
Robinson
is born.

1919　　1929　　1936

October 29
"Black Tuesday" marks
the beginning of the
Great Depression
in America.

July 26
President Harry Truman
signs an executive
order mandating the
integration of the
US military.

1947　　1948　　1949

April 15
Jackie debuts with
the Brooklyn Dodgers
and becomes the first
black player in Major
League Baseball since
1887. He wins the
first ever Rookie of
the Year Award.

November 18
Jackie wins
the National
League Most
Valuable
Player Award.

September 1
Germany, led by Adolf
Hitler and the Nazi Party,
invades Poland. Great
Britain and France declare
war on Hitler's Nazi state,
starting World War II.

October 23
Jackie Robinson
signs a contract
to play for
the Montreal
Royals.

1939　　1941　　　1945

December 7
The United
States enters
World War II
after Japan
bombs the US
naval station at
Pearl Harbor,
Hawaii.

September 2
World War II
comes to
an official
end.

May 17
The US Supreme
Court orders
the integration
of public
schools
across the
country.

1954　　　1955

October 4
The Dodgers play
their eighth
World Series and
get their first
victory, their
only one in
Brooklyn.

December 1
Rosa Parks
refuses to give
up her seat on a
bus in Montgomery,
Alabama, and is
arrested.

November 13
The Supreme
Court rules that
segregation of public
transportation is
unconstitutional,
ending the practice
nationwide.

January 5
Jackie Robinson
officially retires
from baseball. He
becomes an executive
for a coffee-shop chain
and a fund-raiser
for the NAACP.

1956

1957

September 4
In Little Rock,
Arkansas, nine
black students
are prevented
from entering the
previously all-white
school by local law
enforcement.

July 2
President Lyndon
B. Johnson signs
the Civil Rights
Act, which outlaws
discrimination by
race, nationality,
and religion.

1964

1968

April 4
Martin Luther King Jr.
is murdered in
Memphis.

April 11
President Johnso
signs the Civil
Rights Act of
1968, which bans
discrimination i
housing.

July 23
Jackie Robinson
is elected to
the Baseball Hall
of Fame in his
first year of
eligibility.

August 28
Jackie Robinson and
his family march with
Martin Luther King Jr.
in Washington, DC,
where King delivers
his "I Have a Dream"
speech.

1962

1963

1972

October 24
Jackie dies at
ome at the age of 53
ue to complications
rom diabetes, which
ad plagued him for
many years.

Further Reading

→ *Civil Rights Then and Now: A Timeline of the Fight for Equality in America* by Kristina Brooke Daniele (Wendybird Press, 2018)

→ *The Hero Two Doors Down* by Sharon Robinson (Scholastic, 2016)

→ *I Have a Dream* by Martin Luther King, Jr., illustrated by Kadir Nelson (Schwartz & Wade Books, 2012)

→ *In the Year of the Boar and Jackie Robinson* by Bette Bao Lord (HarperCollins Children's Books, 1986)

→ *March* (Books One, Two, and Three) by John Lewis and Andrew Aydin (Top Shelf Productions, 2013, 2015, 2016)

Websites

→ baseballhall.org

The official website of the National Baseball Hall of Fame.

→ https://www.mlb.com/player/jackie-robinson-121314

The official Major League Baseball website, including statistics and awards from Jackie Robinson's baseball career.

Glossary

bigotry: Being intolerant toward people who have different opinions or characteristics.

boycott: An organized, public decision to stop using a good or service.

bullpen: A place on a baseball field where pitchers warm up before they start pitching.

civil rights: The rights to fair and equal treatment in all aspects of life.

color line: A barrier preventing people of color from taking part in various activities with white people.

diabetes: A disease that causes a person's blood sugar level to become too high.

heritage: A person's background.

<u>Glossary</u>

hit (in baseball): An act or instance of a player reaching base safely after putting the ball in play.

integration: The process of ending the enforced separation of people by race.

Jim Crow: The term for a variety of laws in the Southern United States between the 1860s and 1960s that stated where black people could live, work, go to school, recreate, eat, drink, and even use the bathroom.

pennant (in baseball): The league championship of the American League or the National League. The two pennant winners play in the World Series.

protest: An organized demonstration meant to bring public attention to an injustice or problem.

rookie (in baseball): A first-year player.

<u>Glossary</u>

segregation: The separation of people by race or religion, especially when enforced by law.

slump (in baseball): When a player does not play up to his or her normal ability for a stretch of several days or longer. (Entire teams can also have slumps.)

statistics/stats (in baseball): Measurements of everything a player accomplishes in games, such as hits, runs scored, runs batted in, and errors committed. Advanced statistics, called sabermetrics, include on-base percentage and total bases.

stocks and shares: A small part of a company. The owner of the stock gets a small percentage of the company's profits.

Index

A

Aaron, Henry, 115

Alexander, Ted, 68

Allies, 57

Alston, Walt, 119–120

American League, 104–105, 155

army, 58–67

  training, 60–61

awards

  Most Valuable Player, 111

  Rookie of the Year, 106

B

Bankhead, Dan, 105

Banks, Ernie, 115

Baseball Hall of Fame, 38, 72, 130–131, 141–142, 151

baseball players, 4–5, 6, 8–9, 10–12, 38–39, 70–75, 92–93, 105

  black, 4–5, 6, 8–9, 10–12, 70–75, 104, 107, 115, 119–120

basketball, 35, 37, 41, 43, 46, 53–54, 56

"beanball," 110

Black, Joe, 115

Black Panthers (US Army), 65

Black Tuesday, 31–32, 150

Boseman, Chadwick, 140

Boston Braves, 2

Boston Red Sox, 39

boxing, 60

Brooklyn Dodgers, 2–3, 8–9, 72–73, 82–83, 87–100, 102–103, 105–112, 113–115, 119–124

buses

  boycotting, 63

  military, 62

  segregation on, 45, 62–63, 78

C

Campanella, Roy, 89, 106, 115

Cannon, Jimmy, 95

Chandler, Happy, 89

Chapman, Ben, 93–94, 96–98

Chock Full o'Nuts, 124–125

civil rights, 63, 126–127, 131, 133–134, 152

Index

Cleveland Indians, 38, 72,
   105, 136
Cobb, Ty, 6, 103
color line, 10, 39, 92, 100, 102
Colvin, Claudette, 63

D
Detroit Tigers, 6
diabetes, 136, 151
dodgeball, 24
Durocher, Leo, 90

E
Ebbets Field, 2, 91, 93, 145
Erskine, Carl, 110

F
football, 17, 24, 34–35, 37,
   41–42, 45, 46, 48, 50,
   53–54, 56, 58, 60–61, 143
Frick, Ford, 97

G
Gold Dust Trio, 50–52
Gordon, Jack, 45
Great Depression, 32, 150

H
Hitler, Adolf, 39, 69, 150
Honolulu Bears, 58
Hopper, Clay, 88
Howard, Elston, 118

I
integration, 8, 11, 89, 92, 115,
   128, 131, 135, 150, 154
Irvin, Monte, 115
Isum, Rachel, *see* Robinson,
   Rachel

J
Jackie Robinson Day, 139
Jackie Robinson Foundation,
   141
jail, 15, 27–28, 48, 50
Jim Crow laws, 14–15, 23, 62,
   69, 78, 84, 90, 155
journalism, 12, 97, 108, 111

K
Kansas City
   Monarchs,
   68, 142

Index

King, Martin Luther, Jr., 126–
127, 131–133, 150–151
Koufax, Sandy, 119–120

L

Lemon, Bob, 38
Little Rock, Arkansas, 128, 151
Los Angeles, California, 16–17,
35, 48, 58, 124
Louis, Joe, 60
Louisville Colonels, 87, 99

M

Madden, Bill, 115
marbles, 24
Mays, Willie, 115–116, 118
Montgomery Bus Boycott, 63
Montreal Royals, 73, 82–83,
87, 91, 151
Muir Technical High School,
36, 41

N

National Association for the
Advancement of Colored
People (NAACP), 8, 127, 151

National League, 92, 97,
104–105, 155
Negro League, 6, 9, 68–70,
73, 80, 105, 107, 142
New York Post, 95, 125
New York Yankees, 6, 38,
105, 112, 113–115, 118,
120–121, 123, 138–139
Newark Little Giants, 4–5
Newcombe, Don, 89, 115

O

Olympics, 19, 35–36, 39,
53, 150
O'Malley, Walter, 119
O'Neil, Buck, 141–142
Owens, Jesse, 39–40

P

Pafko, Andy, 113
Paige, Leroy "Satchel," 70–72,
75, 106
Parks, Rosa, 63, 126
Pasadena, California,
16–17, 20, 26, 28, 31,
33–34, 40, 42–43, 47, 64,
66, 76, 124, 143

Index

Pearl Harbor, 58, 149

pennants, 104, 112–113, 120, 123, 155

Pepper Street, 17, 21, 26

"Pepper Street Gang," 26, 28, 33, 36, 46

playoffs, 104, 113

police, 25–28, 47, 64, 98
    arrested by, 48, 64

Providence Grays, 4

R

racism, 5, 7–8, 26–28, 40, 45–46, 50, 61–64, 73, 78, 80, 86–89, 90, 92–98, 110, 118, 128–129

Reese, Pee Wee, 99, 143

Rickey, Branch, 8–10, 73–74, 76, 81, 82, 86–89, 90–91, 94, 98–99, 105, 109, 119, 133, 137

Rivera, Mariano "Mo," 138–139

Robinson, David, 134

Robinson, Edgar, 18, 25, 33

Robinson, Frank, 19, 33, 36, 48, 49, 136

Robinson, Jackie, Jr., 134

Robinson, Mack, 18–19, 22, 34–36, 39–40, 42–43, 48, 143, 151

Robinson, Mallie, 16–23, 25, 33, 78

Robinson, Rachel, 54–56, 66, 70, 74, 76, 78–80, 84–86, 90, 95, 98, 141

Robinson, Sharon, 134, 140

Robinson, Willa Mae, 19

rookies, 2, 72, 82, 95, 106, 115, 119, 121, 138, 157

Roosevelt, Franklin D., 57, 68

Rose Bowl, 17, 34, 143

Ruth, Babe, 6, 140

S

scholarships, 48, 141

segregation, 7, 63, 68, 88, 127, 138, 150

slavery, 14, 23

soccer, 24

spring training, 76–77, 80, 82, 89, 91, 110

Stanky, Eddie, 94–95

Index

Stengel, Casey, 115

stock market crash, 31–32

Stovey, George, 5

Strode, Woody, 50

Sukeforth, Clyde, 73

T

Thompson, Hank, 107

Thomson, Bobby, 113

Toledo Blue Stockings, 4

track and field, 34–36, 41–43,
  53–54

Truman, Harry, 68, 147

U

university, 48, 50, 53, 56,
  60–61

W

Walker, Dixie, 90

Walker, Moses Fleetwood, 4

Washington, Kenny, 50

White, William Edward, 4

Williams, Ted, 38–39

World Series, 38, 72, 104–105,
  112, 113, 120–123, 152, 157

World War II, 8, 53, 93,
  152–153

FOLLOW THE TRAIL!

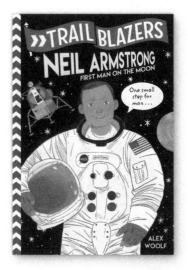

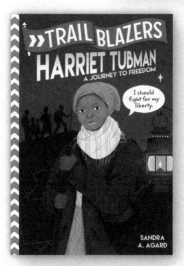

TURN THE PAGE FOR A SNEAK PEEK AT THESE TRAILBLAZERS BIOGRAPHIES!

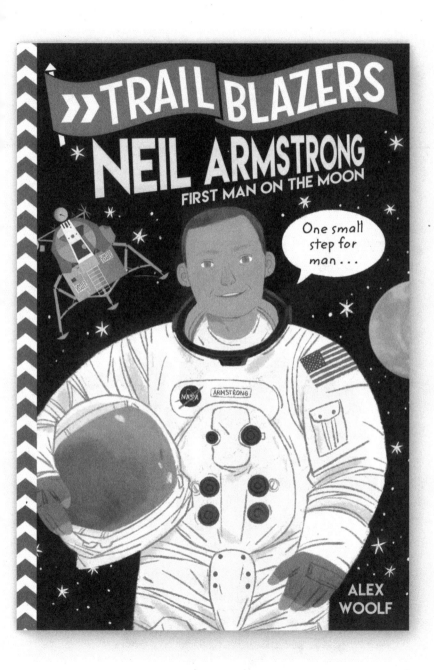

⇟ FLYING LESSONS ⇞

Airplanes remained Neil's first love. His dream was to become both a pilot and an aeronautical engineer—someone who designs and builds planes. About three or four miles outside Wapakoneta was Port Koneta Airport. Neil cycled or hitchhiked there as often as he could to watch the planes land and take off, and talk to the pilots.

When he was fifteen, Neil began saving up for flying lessons. He got a job at Rhine and Brading's Pharmacy, where he earned forty cents an hour. A one-hour flying lesson cost nine dollars, so he had to work twenty-two and a half hours to pay for one lesson! Neil supplemented his earnings at the pharmacy by offering to wash down the airplanes at Port Koneta. He even helped the airport mechanics with some routine maintenance work, servicing the planes' cylinders, pistons, and valves.

Eventually, Neil had saved up enough money to pay for some lessons. A veteran army pilot named Aubrey Knudegard taught him. They flew in a light, high-wing monoplane called an Aeronca Champion.

<u>Aircraft Fact File</u>

Name: Aeronca Champion
Nickname: "Champ"
Length: 21.5 ft. (6.6 m)
Wingspan: 35.2 ft. (10.7 m)
Engine: 65 horsepower
Top speed: 100 mph (161 kmh)
First flight: April 29, 1944

Project Gemini

The purpose of Project Gemini was to develop space-travel techniques that would be needed for the Apollo program, which aimed to land astronauts on the moon. Two of the critical techniques that needed to be developed were:

- extra-vehicular activity (EVA)— when astronauts leave the spacecraft in their spacesuits to work outside it

- space rendezvous and docking—when two spacecraft join together in orbit

BECOMING AN ASTRONAUT

Two months earlier, Mercury astronaut John Glenn had become the first American to orbit Earth. His achievement had captured the public imagination like nothing since Charles Lindbergh's famous transatlantic flight in 1927. Neil saw there was real excitement surrounding NASA's space program, and he wondered if he should be part of it. However, he delayed sending in his application and missed the June 1 deadline by about a week.

Luckily, a man named Dick Day was one of the people in charge of selecting the new astronauts. He had worked with Neil at Edwards, and he thought him better qualified than anyone to be an astronaut. When Neil's application came in, Day slipped it into the pile with all the other applications so no one would realize it was late. In September 1962, Neil was thrilled to learn that he had been selected as one of the new astronauts.

⋚ WALKING ON THE MOON ⋚

Buzz soon followed Neil out, and the two of them explored the lunar surface. "It has a stark beauty all its own," remarked Neil. Buzz described it as "magnificent desolation." The powdery soil was quite slippery, they discovered, but walking was no problem. They unveiled a commemorative plaque that had been mounted on *Eagle*'s base.

They planted a US flag, stiffened with wire to make it look like it was flying in a breeze. Neil photographed Buzz saluting it.

President Richard Nixon called them by radio-telephone from the White House. "This certainly has to be the most historic telephone call ever made," he said. "I just can't tell you how proud we all are of what you've done.... For one priceless moment in the whole history of man, all the people of this Earth are truly one."

Neil and Buzz spent the rest of the EVA collecting rock and soil samples and performing experiments. They set up devices to sense moonquakes and to measure the distance between the moon and Earth. Those devices would stay on the moon.

≛ BEASTS AT THE BIRCHES ≛

Despite the war, Jane spent many happy years at the Birches. To her delight, the house had a large, rambling garden, where she played for hours on end. Jane's favorite tree was a big beech tree. She loved it so much that Danny gave it to her, officially, for her tenth birthday. Jane was often found perched on a branch of her tree, reading a book or doing her homework.

Jane also collected a large number of pets, including a tortoise called Johnny Walker, a slow worm called Solomon, a canary called Peter, not to mention several terrapins, guinea pigs, and cats. Jane and Judy also had their own "racing" snails with numbers painted on their shells. The girls kept the snails in a wooden box covered with a piece of glass and with no bottom, so that the snails could feed on fresh dandelion leaves as the girls moved the box around the lawn.

Animal Fact File

Name: Peter

Animal: Canary

Behavior: Slept in a cage
            but was free to
            fly around during the day.

⋝ THE ALLIGATOR CLUB ⋝

As well as watching the birds, squirrels,
foxes, insects, and spiders that came
into the garden, Jane started her own
nature club. It was called the Alligator Club and had
four members—Jane; Judy; and their two best friends,
Sally and Sue Cary, who came to stay at the Birches
during the summer breaks. Each girl had to choose

an animal as her code name—
Jane was Red Admiral, Sally
was Puffin, Sue was Ladybird,
and Judy was Trout.

Primate, Monkey, or Ape?

There are more than three hundred species of primates. They all share many features, including large brains compared to the size of their bodies, forward-facing eyes, and flexible limbs and hands for grasping. But, while monkeys and apes (chimps, bonobos, gorillas, orangutans, and gibbons) are both primates, monkeys are not the same as apes. Here's how to tell them apart:

APES

Larger brains

Shoulders designed for swinging from branch to branch

Larger bodies and broader chests

No tails

MONKEYS

Bodies built for running across branches, not swinging

Smaller brains

Smaller bodies and narrower chests

Most have tails

Over the next few months, Jane's frustration grew. Sometimes, she didn't see any chimps for days, and when she did, she couldn't get close enough to observe them properly. So as not to startle the chimps, Jane wore clothes that blended in with the forest, and sat patiently for hours. The minute she tried to move nearer, the chimps scampered off. She was getting worried that if she didn't get results soon, Leakey would have to cancel the project, and she would have to leave Gombe.

Sweater

Food and drink

Notebook and pens

BEANS BEANS

Binoculars

Sleeping bag

Bagged lunch

⋛ HARRIET'S ESCAPE ⋚

That night, Harriet went about her usual chores. John was hardly speaking to her these days, and they spent most evenings in silence. When she knew John was sound asleep, she got up quietly and helped herself to some ash cake (a type of bread), a piece of salt herring, and her wedding quilt.

Rather than set off into the woods, Harriet decided to head for Bucktown to the farm on the edge of the town. She was going to ask that white woman she had met by the road for assistance. It was a risky move—although the woman had said she'd help, Harriet couldn't know whether she'd really meant it, or how committed she would be to her offer once she discovered that Harriet was a runaway.

She uttered a quick prayer, walked toward the woman's door, and gently tapped on it. In the stillness of the night, the knock sounded so loud. The door opened, and the Quaker woman appeared. To Harriet's great relief, the woman nodded and asked Harriet to come in. She led Harriet into the kitchen and told her to sit down. She wrote two names on a piece of paper, then gave Harriet directions of where to go next.

The first stop, or station, on the Underground
Railroad was another farm; Harriet couldn't miss it—
there were two white posts with round knobs on them.
The people there would give her food and clothing and
keep her safe until it was time to move to the next place.

⇉ FAME AND FORTUNE ⇇

As she grew more famous, it became difficult for Harriet
to make as many trips down South as before. Still
desperate to help the Underground Railroad's efforts, in
1858 she began lecturing at locations all over the North.
Her firsthand accounts of the Underground Railroad
and its workings proved very popular, and she raised
even more money to help fugitives, station masters, and
conductors fighting to free slaves.

    She was invited to speak in the parlor rooms of high
society in Concord and Boston. In these anti-slavery
speeches, Harriet told fascinating stories of her
narrow escapes. Money poured in as more and more
people heard about her amazing rescues.

⇉ HARRIET'S STORIES ⇇

One time, Harriet was traveling during the day in
her home state of Maryland. She was wearing a
large sunbonnet and kept her head bowed, but when
she passed a former employer, Harriet worried that
she would be recognized. Luckily, she'd just bought
a couple of chickens at the market.

Thinking quickly, she opened the cage of chickens, which fluttered and squawked, causing an awful noise and diverting attention from herself.

On a different occasion, Harriet was traveling in a railway coach and noticed two gentlemen quietly discussing whether she was the woman on the Wanted poster at the station. Never one to panic, she simply picked up a newspaper and began to "read" it. Harriet Tubman was known to be illiterate—so this woman reading the paper studiously surely could not be the fugitive!

COMING SOON . . .

>>TRAIL BLAZERS

Albert Einstein

Beyoncé

Stephen Hawking

J. K. Rowling